Carve
your clay

Carve
your clay

TECHNIQUES TO BRING THE
POTTERY SURFACE TO LIFE

Hilda Carr

Search Press

A QUARTO BOOK

First published in 2020 by
Search Press Ltd
Wellwood
North Farm Road
Tunbridge Wells
Kent TN2 3DR

Reprinted 2021

ISBN: 978-1-78221-852-4

Conceived, edited and designed by
Quarto Publishing plc, an imprint of
The Quarto Group
The Old Brewery
6 Blundell Street
London N7 9BH

www.quartoknows.com
QUAR.333741

Commissioning editor: Lily de Gatacre
Copy editor: Caroline West
Proofreader: Julia Shone
Photographers: Hilda Carr, David Carr,
 Olivia Bull
Designer: Jackie Palmer
Senior art editor: Emma Clayton
Art director: Gemma Wilson
Senior commissioning editor: Eszter Karpati
Publisher: Samantha Warrington

Printed in China

Contents

Meet Hilda

I started a ceramics course one rainy Saturday in November and I was hooked straight away.

When everything else in life is so hectic – when we only feel productive if we've managed to cross twenty things off our to-do list – pottery for me was the antidote. There is something so calmingly simple about taking a lump of earth and slowly shaping it with your hands into something beautiful. The process of carving into clay has a definite meditative quality: it's slow, it's measured and it requires your full attention. It appeals to me as much for the aesthetic that it gives to a piece as the pleasure that I get from making it.

I remember, at one of my first pottery classes, spending the majority of the lesson hunched over a workbench with a clay bowl in front of me, slowly but carefully carving an intricate texture into the surface. I found the process so absorbing that when I stepped out of the studio at the end of the lesson and into the fresh air, it literally felt like I was landing back on planet Earth; it was as if for a couple of hours at least I could forget everything else.

I hope the projects in this book inspire you to create your own carved pieces and that the techniques, and the results they produce, bring as much joy to you as they do to me.

01/Basics

In this chapter you'll find information on the basic elements to consider before you start making your carved piece. Hilda will introduce you to her essential carving tools and discuss which clay is best for creating carved pieces – and what state it should be in. You'll also find an overview of the carving techniques that are covered in the book, and which projects you will find them in.

Clays for Carving

In my own work I primarily use stoneware clay. It is perfect for carving. It's very strong, waterproof and is durable enough to be used for everyday pieces.

There are many different types of stoneware to choose from – from very smooth to heavily grogged. A clay that is grogged has very small pieces of fired clay mixed into the clay body. Grog can help add stability, particularly to hand-built pieces, and can also add a wonderful rough texture, giving an extra dimension to your piece.

The clay that you choose for your carved piece will depend on the technique and tools that you're using, as well as the overall look and feel that you want to achieve. A smooth clay creates a perfect backdrop for those pieces where you want the focus to be the surface design – it allows you to create fine lines and detail and let the pattern really sing. If it's all about the texture then you can get some wonderful tactile effects with a grogged clay. For tiles and other hand-built pieces, look for clays that are specially formulated for this purpose. They generally have less plasticity, making them less prone to warping.

THE STATE OF CLAY

When you make a piece of pottery, the clay goes through a drying process; from soft and malleable when the piece is formed, to bone dry when all the moisture has evaporated and it's ready for firing. In between these two states is a stage known as 'leather-hard'. This is the most important stage when it comes to carving clay and the success of your carved piece will depend heavily on you catching it at just the right time. Leather-hard is the point at which the clay is still pliable but no longer tacky to the touch. When clay is at this stage it is robust enough to be handled without risk of warping the shape but still supple enough to allow for sections of clay to be carved away or detail to be added.

Within the leather-hard stage there is a bit of wiggle room, however. Sgraffito, for example, is more effective when the clay is on the drier side of leather-hard – but not yet bone dry – as we just want to scrape away the top layer of slip rather than cut into the clay. (Sgraffito means 'scratched away' in Italian.) Techniques that require larger tools, such as faceting, are best done when the clay is on the softer side – still slightly tacky to the touch – to allow the tool to cut through large sections of clay easily.

Within each project I will give you tips on what stage the clay should be at before you begin carving.

Smooth clay

Lightly grogged clay

Heavily grogged clay

TOO WET

If the clay is too wet, the carved pieces will stick to the pot as you try to remove them and you won't get a clean finish. You'll also risk warping your pot as it won't be stable enough to handle at this stage.

TOO DRY

If the clay is too dry, the tool will scratch into the clay rather than cut into it. You'll have to apply so much pressure that you'll risk cracking or warping your pot.

JUST RIGHT

When you get your clay in just the right leather-hard state, the tool cuts through the clay smoothly and the carved pieces come away easily.

Tools for Carving

My collection of carving tools is always expanding. I love experimenting with new tools and discovering new ways to achieve a particular look or effect. Here, we're going to look specifically at the tools needed to carve into clay rather than general pottery tools.

Don't limit yourself to purchasing specialist pottery tools; a number of my tools are either home-made or re-purposed items from around the house. And never forget the most important tools at your disposal – your hands! You can soften down carved lines and edges by wetting your thumb or finger and smoothing over the lines. Depending on how subtle you want your carving to appear, you can simply apply less or more pressure to get your desired effect.

A great way to get an idea of what effects you can achieve with your tools is to roll out a large slab of clay, leave it to firm up slightly and then have fun experimenting. Try using the same tool in different ways: use the side or back of the tool; apply less pressure or more; create a sense of movement with a sweep of your arm; or use a straight edge to help you create an intricate, geometric pattern.

LOOKING AFTER YOUR TOOLS

Remember that carving tools will get blunt over time. You can sharpen them with a file or a Dremel tool. Cleaning and drying them carefully after each use will increase their longevity.

HILDA'S ESSENTIAL CARVING TOOLS

1. CHEESE SLICE
This works just like a potter's wire but the central bar of the tool prevents the wire from cutting too deeply. This is a great tool for faceting.

2 & 3. SGRAFFITO TOOLS
There are lots of different tools available for sgraffito work. These are two of my favourites: a small ball-tipped tool (2), great for making fine lines and a scoop tool (3), which you can either use on its side for scraping larger areas or use the fine point for creating detailed designs.

4–7. LOOP TOOLS
My absolute favourites and the first carving tools I ever bought. These come in all shapes and sizes with rounded tips, straight-edged tips or pointed tips. These are great tools for fluting, creating texture and cutting in sharp-angled shapes.

8. FLEXIBLE STEEL KIDNEY-SHAPED RIB
This is a useful tool for scraping larger areas and for carving shallow curves. It works best on drier clay.

9 & 10. COMBING TOOLS
Use a specialist potter's tool (10) or you can easily create your own by cutting a design into an old credit card (9).

11. POTTER'S KNIFE
This is a must-have potter's tool – for carving and for general use – and they come in all shapes and sizes. I like this long-bladed version as it's great for incising and fettling.

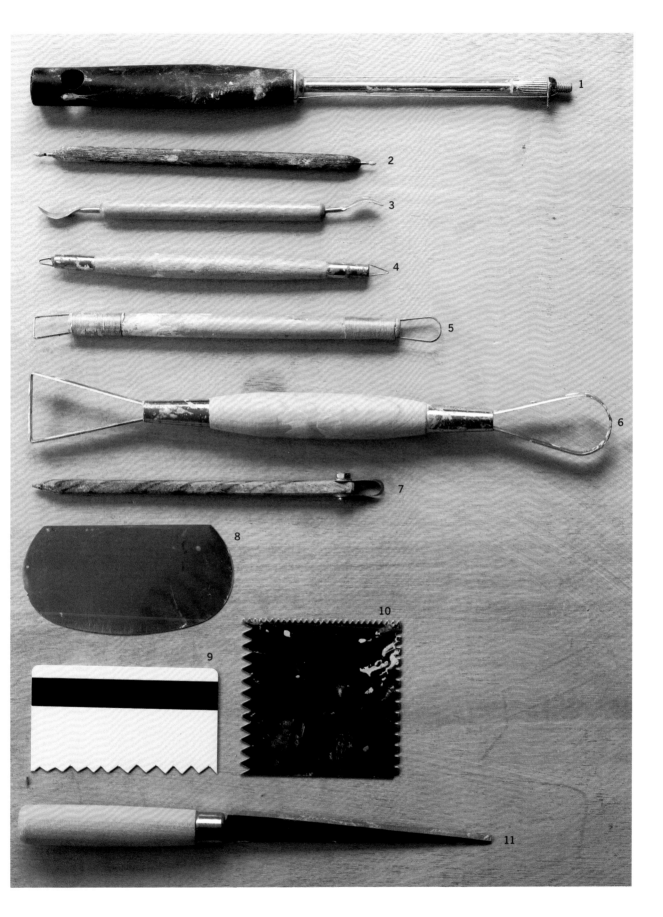

Forming

Carving techniques can be applied to any vessel regardless of how the piece was formed. In my own work, I throw most of my pieces on the potter's wheel. And as a thrower first and foremost, many of the projects in this book start with thrown forms.

In the projects in this book, you will also find some hand-building, pinching, slip-casting and slump moulding. Most of the projects can be adapted to suit your favoured way of working.

The main consideration, however you form your vessel, is to make sure you allow some extra thickness in your walls. Depending on the technique, sometimes large parts of the vessel will be cut away so give yourself some extra clay to work with.

THROWING

Thrown forms create a great canvas for carving projects. You can even use the potter's wheel itself as an additional tool to create interesting effects; using the spinning of the wheel to exaggerate or add movement to carving, as in the Bellied Bowl project on pages 126–131.

HAND-BUILDING

Creating a hand-built piece means you can add your carved design to a flat slab of clay before construction. The Impressed Mini Planter on pages 82–89 involves rolling a slab of clay over a design carved into linoleum, an effect you couldn't achieve with a thrown form.

PINCHING

A pinch pot can have a more organic quality than a thrown vessel – embrace the quirks and character of this type of form by introducing a less restrained style of carving that adds to this free-form way of working.

SLIP-CASTING

You can create interesting carving effects with a slip-cast piece; taking advantage of the ability to construct your pot with multiple layers of different coloured slip, then carving through them to reveal a design.

SLUMP-MOULDING

A form made with a slump mould is simple to carve as the shape is supported by the mould as you work on it. A slump mould exposes the interior of a vessel as the clay is laid into a concave shape. A hump mould is the opposite, with the clay laid onto a convex shape leaving the exterior exposed.

Carving Techniques

The effects that you can achieve with a simple carving tool are limitless. Combine that with the number of possibilities for form, clay type and glaze and you've got enough options to make sure you never get bored!

The projects that I've included in this book are designed to introduce you to just some of the ways you can bring your ceramic pieces to life through carving. Some are very simple, requiring only your hands and a loop tool, others are a little more complicated, requiring a few more tools and techniques. Use them as a starting point to explore and develop your own designs – create your own unique versions that embrace your style and preferred way of working.

As with anything, confidence comes with practice, so don't be afraid to make mistakes. I remember the first time I tried carving: I had made a small bowl on the potter's wheel that I was very proud of – successes at this stage being still few and far between. I wanted to carve a simple design into the outside of the bowl but I was terrified of cutting into it and ruining the whole thing. It took a few attempts to achieve the look I wanted, but I found the more I practised, the more I gained a feel of how the clay would respond, and with it a little more confidence.

The joy of hand-made ceramics comes from knowing that a piece is one of a kind, it is not about achieving perfection. The marks of the maker: the hand-drawn lines, fingerprints and marks that show how the piece was constructed add the character and individuality that you can't get from a mass-produced piece. Don't worry about getting your lines perfectly parallel or your shapes completely symmetrical. Embrace these quirks: it's these that make it yours and completely unique.

HEALTH AND SAFETY

- *Always wear a respiratory mask when making up slips or glazes, sanding bisque-ware or in any instance where you're dealing with dry ingredients.*
- *When using a technique where the clay needs to be on the drier side, always brush away the carved clay rather than blow.*

KEY TECHNIQUES

These are the carving techniques that you will find covered by the projects in this book. Each one creates a different effect, so try a few out and find out which best suits your aesthetic and preferred way of working.

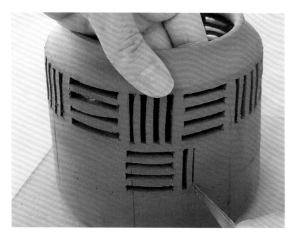

INCISING

Use a potter's knife to cut a pattern right through the wall of your vessel. This technique is great for candle holders as the pattern will be projected around the room when the candle is lit. Project: Incised Candle Holder, pages 68–73.

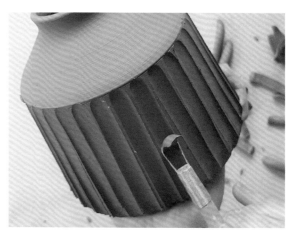

FLUTING

Use a loop tool to cut ribbons of clay down the length of a pot. You can get a variety of effects depending on the size and shape of your chosen tool. Project: Fluted Stem Vase, pages 60–65.

CARVING A GEOMETRIC PATTERN

Mark out a rough pattern on your piece before carving your design. This technique can add a great architectural quality and the design can be as simple or as intricate as you want. Project: Geometric Carved Tile, pages 26–29.

COMBING

Use the teeth of a combing tool to carve narrow, parallel grooves into the clay, which add surface texture and interest. I use this tool with the pot still on the wheel to help get accurate lines. Project: Combed Mug, pages 44–51.

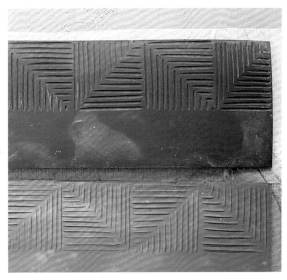

CREATING TEXURE

There are lots of options to create surface interest and detail with a variety of loop tools. Work freehand and let your imagination loose. Projects: Textured Bowl, pages 38–43 and Contrast-Carved Planter, pages 54–59.

IMPRESSING

Carve a design into a piece of craft linoleum and then impress your clay into it. This technique works best on slab-built pieces. Project: Impressed Mini Planter, pages 82–89.

INLAYING

Carve out narrow grooves with a fine tool, then fill them with a coloured slip. Your design is revealed when the slip has hardened and the excess is scraped away. Project: Inlaid Storage Jar, pages 108–115.

GIVING SHAPE TO A FORM

I use this technique on wheel-thrown pieces to carve sharp angles out of a solid piece of clay. Project: Angle-Carved Candlestick, pages 102–105.

MIDWAY THROWING

Carve a design into a freshly thrown cylinder then belly out the shape to contort and stretch the carved lines. This adds an organic, less refined feel to the piece. Project: Bellied Bowl, pages 126–131.

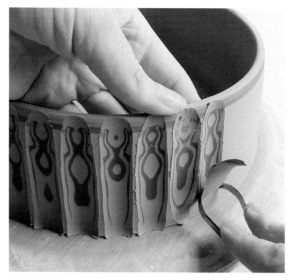

CARVING MARBLED SURFACE

Marble two coloured clays together then reveal the pattern when you carve through the surface. Project: Agateware Serving Bowl, pages 132–139.

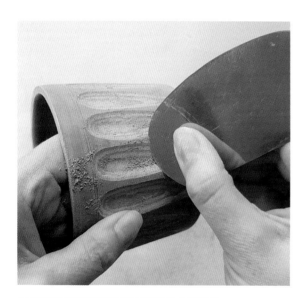

CARVING THROUGH COLOURED LAYERS

Build up coloured layers of clay by pouring stained casting slip into a plaster mould. The colours are revealed as you scrape away the layers. Project: Slip-Cast Beaker, pages 116–123.

FACETING

Use a wire or knife to slice away flat strips of clay. Choosing a straight wire or wiggle wire will create different effects. Project: Faceted Jug, pages 74–79.

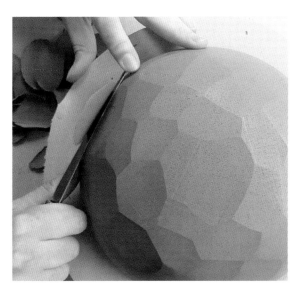

FETTLING

Trim the edges of a piece with a knife, in this case trimming the edges of a curve to create a multi-faceted shape. Project: Fettled Hanging Planter, pages 96–101.

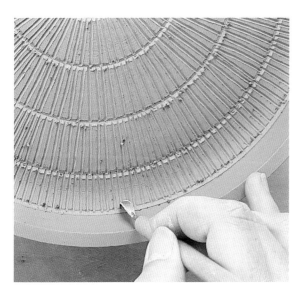

SGRAFFITO

Carve away a top layer of coloured slip to reveal the clay beneath. Projects: Sgraffito Vase, pages 30–34 and Sgraffito Serving Plate, pages 90–95.

Notes on Glazing

When it comes to glazing, I like to keep things simple. I want the focus to be on the carving itself, so I choose finishes that complement rather than try to compete.

I tend to stick to a limited colour palette of whites, greys, blues and blacks, using light glazes that emphasize the pattern or texture. Like every part of the creative process, it's best to experiment and to find the style and processes that work best for you. There are so many colours and types of glazes for you to try and find what is right for you.

FIRING
All projects have been bisque fired to cone 06 and glaze fired to cone 6 in an electric kiln.

You can use glazes to enhance a carved piece in many different ways:
- Try translucent glazes that leave the qualities of the clay still visible underneath.
- Use a transparent glaze to add vibrancy to the colour of a sgraffito or inlaid design.
- Use glazes that collect and pool in carved divots to emphasize texture.
- Use glazes that break on carved and raised lines to accentuate a pattern.
- Build up layers of slips or washes to add subtle colour and interest.
- Use a glaze colour that contrasts with the colour of the clay. A white glaze on a black clay, for example.
- Nothing at all –just let the beauty of the raw clay speak for itself.

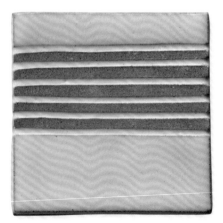

A gloss white glaze contrasting with raw clay.

A translucent, matt white glaze that breaks over the raised details.

(Left) A matt transparent glaze that brings out the vivid colour of the slip.

(Right) A clay body with large flecks of iron shines through a white glaze.

 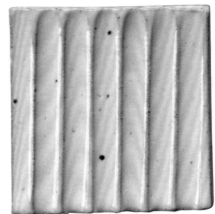

(Left) Layered copper slip and a translucent white glaze over a speckled clay body.

(Right) A gloss white glaze that contrasts with the black clay body.

 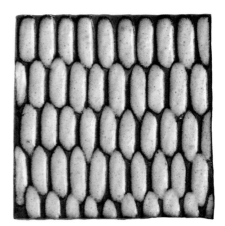

(Left) Unglazed, raw clay.

(Right) A watered-down white glaze applied in several layers that pools in the divots.

02/Projects

This section comprises 16 beautifully carved projects for you to recreate and to be inspired by. Hilda will guide you through the forming of each piece and then give instructions on how to do the carving technique. You'll also find some ideas for how to finish your piece with glazes and slips to further your design.

Geometric Carved Tile

This project is great for beginners and the perfect introduction to carving.
A single tile would make a great trivet or arrange a few to create a piece of wall art.
You could even use them to fulfil a more practical purpose as a sink splashback.

CLAY

Approx. 700g
(1½lb) of buff hand-
building stoneware

TOOLS AND
MATERIALS

For Forming
Thin cardboard
Compass
Ruler
Scissors
Rolling guides
Rolling pin
Rubber kidney-
　shaped rib
Potter's knife

For Carving
Marking tool
Loop tool
Sponge
Sand paper

FIRING

Bisque fired to cone
06 and glaze fired
to cone 6 in an
electric kiln

Flat pieces like this are prone to warping. To help prevent this, make sure you're using a clay suitable for hand-building (this usually has less plasticity than throwing clays, see page 10). Roll your clay out onto a board rather than directly onto your workbench. This way you can move it out of the way easily without having to peel it off the bench. Clay has a memory, so move it as little as possible while it's drying and let it dry slowly under plastic.

Here, I've experimented with a range of geometric designs using some different sized tools. Leaving a portion uncarved will create a stronger overall look when you group your tiles together.

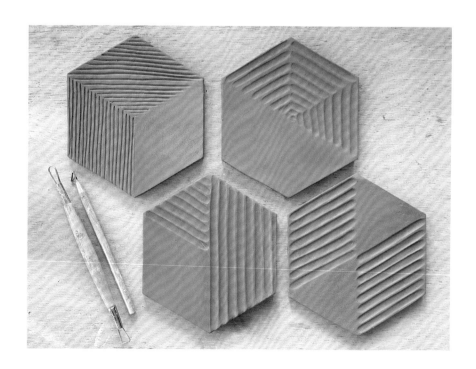

FORMING

This project is for a single tile approximately 18cm (7in) in diameter.

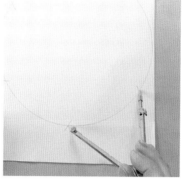

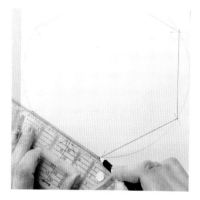

1 Create a cardboard template for your tile by first drawing a circle with a compass. Then, keeping your compass at the same angle, mark six points around the circumference.

2 Connect your marks with a straight edge and cut out the cardboard hexagon.

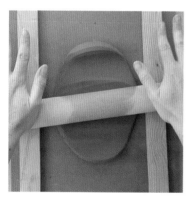

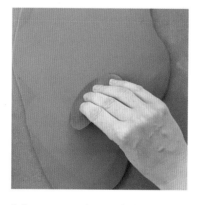

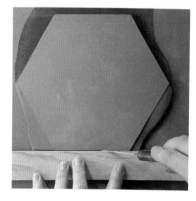

3 Roll a slab of clay to a thickness of 1.25cm (½in) using a rolling pin and guides (or a slab roller if you have one), rolling the clay in all directions.

4 Compress and smooth the surface with a rubber kidney-shaped rib.

5 Place your template on your rolled-out clay (spraying with a little water will help to keep it in place) and cut out using a sharp potter's knife and straight edge.

CARVING

1 Mark a faint line through the centre of the hexagon, then another to divide one of the halves in two.

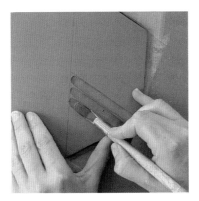

2 Wait until your clay is leather-hard before carving. Following the lines, use your loop tool to carve your design. Support the edge of the tile with your thumb as you carve to prevent the edges chipping off.

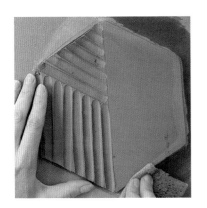

3 Sponge the carved lines and edges of the tile to smooth it off.

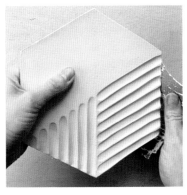

4 After bisque firing, gently sand to remove any burrs.

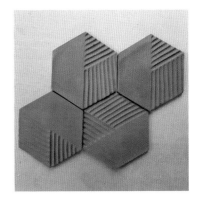

5 These tiles look great in multiples, rotated randomly to form an interesting pattern.

FINISHES

I've glazed this tile half in a matt white and half in a magnetite green. I love the contrast between the earthy carved section and the glossy glaze.

TOP TIPS TO AVOID WARPING

* *Use a clay specially formulated for hand-building.*
* *Roll your clay no thinner than 1.25cm (½in).*
* *Roll the clay in all directions.*
* *Smooth and compress the surface with a rubber kidney-shaped rib.*
* *Don't lift the slab from the board after you've rolled it out.*
* *Try not to handle the tile too much while it's drying.*
* *Make sure it dries slowly and evenly.*
* *If the edges start to curl up slightly, bisque fire it upside down.*

Sgraffito Vase

Sgraffito is one of my absolute favourite carving techniques and one I use a lot in my work. It's defined as a form of decoration made by scratching through a surface to reveal a lower layer of contrasting colour.

CLAY

Approx. 1.4kg
(3lb) of smooth
white stoneware

TOOLS AND MATERIALS

For Forming
Throwing rib
Sponge
Turning tool

For Sgraffito
Coloured slip
Flat brush
Loop tool
Banding wheel
Chalk marker
Sand paper

FIRING

Bisque fired to cone
06 and glaze fired
to cone 6 in an
electric kiln

In this project I've used a vibrant blue slip painted onto the thrown form, which creates a really striking contrast to the white stoneware that is revealed through the carving.

There are infinite options for pattern design here and it's great fun to experiment. I take pattern inspiration from mid-century Scandinavian and West-German ceramics and textiles and I find that sometimes the simplest designs have the most impact. Before creating a piece, I often experiment with pattern on a series of test tiles, each painted with coloured slip (see below).

These vases look great grouped together as a collection with varying shapes, sizes and patterns. They work really well with simple flowers; perhaps just a few stems of something architectural and unfussy that shows off the striking design of the piece.

FORMING

This project is for a basic straight-sided cylinder approximately 25cm (10in) tall.

1 Start by coning and centring the clay on the wheel.

2 Use your thumbs to drill a hole in the centre, then open up the base to the desired width.

3 Start pulling up the walls. Apply more pressure on the outer wall to keep the form from flaring out. Once your cylinder is at the desired height, you can straighten up the walls. The outer walls need to be smooth and free from throwing lines and any bumps, so you can use a wooden rib to smooth them off. This will give a lovely surface for the slip to be applied to.

4 Once the piece is leather-hard, you can turn the bottom. I've given my cylinder a chamfered edge, which you can do with your turning tool.

APPLYING THE SLIP

1 Dampen the wheel head and centre your leather-hard cylinder, right side up, on the wheel. This will keep it in place enough to apply the slip.

2 Use a flat brush and really load it up well with slip. We want the slip to go on smoothly without dragging, so don't be afraid to use a generous amount. Run your brush lightly up and down the side to ensure you've got an even coverage.

The pot will need 2–3 coats of slip. Make sure you leave it to dry slightly in between coats – it needs to be not sticky to the touch before you apply the next coat.

3 Once the final coat of slip is dry, centre your pot back on the wheel head. Use your loop tool to tidy up the lines of the slip. A flat-edged strip tool will help to get a nice crisp edge.

CARVING

1 To create guidelines for carving, I use a dressmakers' hem-marking tool. It puffs a neat horizontal chalk line which can then be easily followed with your carving tool. The chalk lines will burn off in the kiln during firing. Use a banding wheel to easily get round the whole of the pot.

2 Following your chalk guidelines, use the rounded end of your loop tool to cut through the slip. Take care not to cut too deeply! I tend to carve the tops first then turn the pot upside down to finish the cut. That way I can get as neat a cut as possible.

3 Once bisque fired, gently sand the piece to get rid of any burrs.

FINISHES

For my sgraffito work I always apply a simple, transparent glaze. You will find that a gloss glaze creates a different effect, sometimes making the slip appear much darker. Take time to experiment with different combinations until you find a finish you like. Test tiles are useful for this.

Textured Bowl

As well as creating pattern, carving is a great way to add texture to a piece. This is a much less uniform way of working than some of the other projects and I find it very therapeutic to slowly turn a smooth slab of clay into a beautifully textured bowl.

CLAY

Approx. 1.4kg
(3lb) of smooth
buff stoneware –
depending on the
size of your mould.
This mould is 28cm
(11in) in diameter.

TOOLS AND
MATERIALS

For Forming
Plaster slump
  mould
Rolling pin
Rolling guides
Canvas
Rubber kidney-
  shaped rib
Bow wire

For Texturing
Banding wheel
Loop tool
Brush
Sponge

FIRING

Bisque fired to cone
06 and glaze fired
to cone 6 in an
electric kiln

If you're looking for pieces you can create without needing to be proficient on the potter's wheel, then this is a great one. It uses a simple plaster slump mould, which you can buy or make yourself. The advantage of carving a piece that is formed like this is you can keep it in the mould to carve it and therefore don't need to worry about the best way to hold the piece to work on it without distorting the shape. It's also easier to judge how deeply to carve as you're more aware of the thickness of the clay.

You can achieve a range of finished looks with just a simple loop tool, depending on its size and the way in which you apply it to the clay. Experiment with a few test tiles and play around with some ideas. All the patterns below were made with a loop tool.

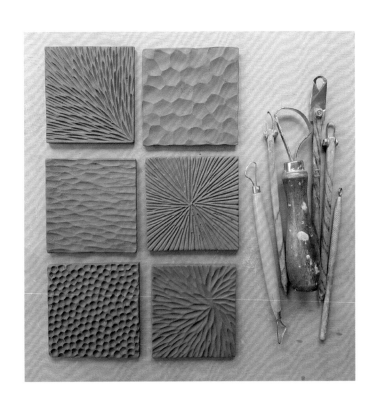

This project is a great opportunity to let out your artistic side with some freehand carving. Rather than focusing on precision or recreating a planned design, just fill the space with beautiful carved marks and concentrate on creating texture.

FORMING

This project is for a bowl with a diameter of approximately 25cm (10in).

1 Make sure your mould is clean by giving it a wipe over with a damp sponge, then leave until completely dry.

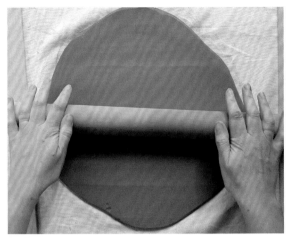

2 Roll out your clay onto a piece of canvas making sure you roll in every direction (this will help prevent warping). Use your rolling guides to achieve an even thickness of approximately 5mm (¼in). Giving the clay a good bash with your rolling pin to flatten it out before you begin will save your arms! Rolling out onto canvas will make it easier to transfer into the mould later on.

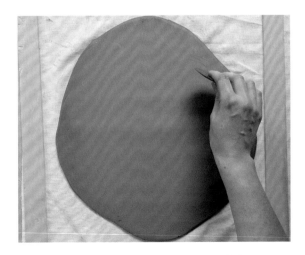

3 Smooth the surface with a flexible rubber kidney-shaped rib. This surface will sit against the plaster mould until the bowl is turned out, so use this opportunity to get a smooth finish while it's easily accessible.

4 Carefully lift your slab – still on the canvas – off the bench, supporting it underneath to prevent the clay from stretching. Gently turn it over and drape it into your mould.

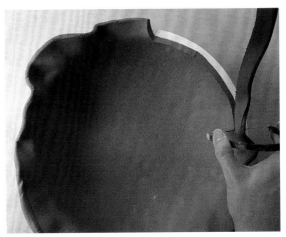

5 Remove the canvas and ease the clay into the curve of the mould by lifting the edges and gently pressing it in from the centre outwards, making sure you don't trap any air.

6 When it's firmly pressed into the mould all the way around, trim off any excess with a wire. I find using a bow wire makes it easy to cut a level line.

7 Smooth over the surface with your rubber kidney-shaped rib. Leave until leather-hard. The plaster will absorb the moisture in the clay so you'll find it dries more quickly than a thrown or hand-built piece.

CARVING

Once your bowl is dry enough, you can begin carving. If you're unsure if your clay is in the right state, try carving a small area. If the clay sticks as you carve, it's not quite dry enough yet; the carved pieces should come away easily. Normally, if the clay feels tacky to the touch it's too wet.

1 In this piece, I started from a single point and carved outwards. I prefer a slightly asymmetrical look so started at one side rather than the centre point. Placing your mould on a banding wheel will make it easier to work with.

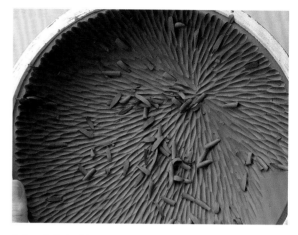

2 Carefully build up your pattern. Your carving doesn't need to be planned too much. It's about creating texture and interest rather than a repeated pattern.

3 Gradually work your way around the bowl. On the rim, I carve right to the edge to create a rough, organic finish.

4 Brush out any loose pieces of clay and give the bowl a smooth over with a damp sponge, following the direction of the pattern, to soften the edges. Don't get rid of these carved pieces of clay; leave them to slake in a jar with some water and you'll have some great slip.

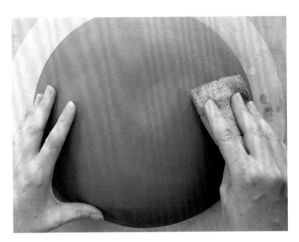

5 Carefully turn the bowl out of the mould then use your sponge to smooth over the exterior of the bowl, removing any imperfections.

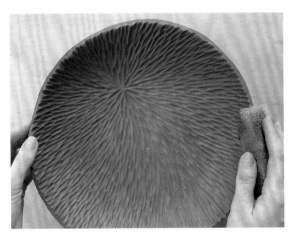

6 Finally, run a sponge around the rim of the bowl then leave to dry completely before bisque firing.

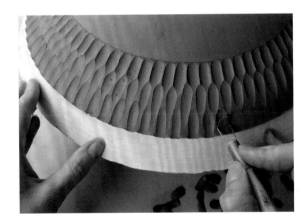

A slump mould is great for creating texture on the inside of a piece. If you wanted to create texture on the outside, you could use a drape or hump mould where the slab of clay is laid over the outside of a form, giving you access to the exterior as the piece dries.

FINISHES

I wanted a very light finish to this piece that would highlight the carved design rather than a heavy glaze that would cover it. Here, I have watered down my usual matt white glaze to about half the usual consistency. Using a jug, pour some glaze into the bowl then swirl it around the inside, taking it up to the edges before tipping it back out into the bucket. Repeat this two or three times, not worrying too much about getting a perfectly even coverage with each pour, but going for a more random effect. The glaze collects in the grooves and picks up the detail of the texture. The exterior of the bowl is left as beautifully tactile raw clay.

Combed Mug

Of all the pieces that I make, my mugs tend to be the most popular. I get lovely feedback from customers telling me how special it is to have a favourite handmade mug that they always reach for. I have many (probably too many!) mugs made by fellow potters that I've collected over the years.

CLAY

Approx. 450g
(1lb) of buff
stoneware

TOOLS AND MATERIALS

For Forming
Straight wooden rib
Cutting-in tool
Turning tool
Potter's knife
Comb for scoring
Slip
Small extruder
Modelling tool
Sand paper

For Combing
Combing tool
Flexible metal
  kidney-shaped rib
Wax emulsion

FIRING

Bisque fired to cone
06 and glaze fired
to cone 6 in an
electric kiln

There really is something special about drinking from a handmade mug and knowing the amount of time and care that has gone into creating it. It turns a rather mundane occurrence into a small daily ritual for me.

I love a mug to be tactile, so that you can really feel the clay when you wrap your hands around it. In this project, I've left a portion of the vessel unglazed and I love the contrast between the rough, raw clay and the smooth, glossy surface of the glaze.

The technique here is quite a simple one but it is the small details that make it stand out. Making sure your combed grooves all line up perfectly and getting precise lines with your glazing will help you to achieve a really neat finish. The key is a steady hand and sharp tools! Remember, if your cut-out design is quite deep, you will need the walls of your mug to be thicker.

You can buy specialist potter's combing tools or you can try making your own. Find some old credit cards and try cutting out your own design (see below). They often work just as well as a specialist tool.

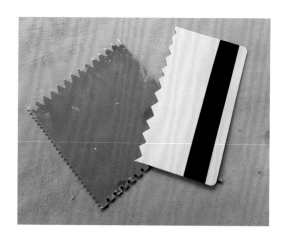

The contrast between the glazed and unglazed portions of this mug, as well as the indentations of the carved areas, make it incredibly tactile and a joy to use.

FORMING

This project is for a mug approximately 10cm (4in) tall.

1 Centre your clay on the wheel by using the heels of your hands to push the clay inwards and upwards to form a cone. Then, push it back down to the wheel head with the side of one hand (a bit like a karate chop) while pushing the side of the clay with the other hand into the centre. Keep your elbows against your body and your weight over the wheel to help control the clay.

2 Supporting the clay with your fingers, use both thumbs to drill a hole in the centre, leaving enough clay at the base to form the bottom of your pot.

3 Now you need to pull your mug out to the right width. With the fingers of your right hand inside the pot and your left hand supporting the outside, gently pull the wall towards you.

4 When pulling up the walls, try to keep your hands in contact with each other as much as possible as it will help you to control the clay. Use a few steady, gentle strokes to pull the walls up. I pull these walls up to around 13cm (5in).

5 Straighten up and smooth off the walls with a wooden rib.

6 Use a cutting-in tool to roughly shape the bottom of the mug. You can define this later when the clay is leather-hard, so it doesn't need to be exact at this stage.

CARVING

To carve this piece it needs to be on the soft side of leather-hard.

1 Secure your mug, right side up, by dampening the wheel head. Keeping one hand inside for support, firmly press your combing tool to the outside. Keeping your elbows locked into your body will help you to keep your hand steady. Notice that I've left the top portion of the mug smooth to make it comfortable to drink from.

2 Turn your mug upside down on the wheel and secure it firmly, then trim off any excess clay on the base.

3 Tidy up where the curve of the base meets the bottom of your combed lines to get a nice neat edge. This will make it much easier to glaze later on.

4 If there are any little burrs on your combed grooves, use a turning tool to clean them up at this stage.

ATTACHING THE HANDLE

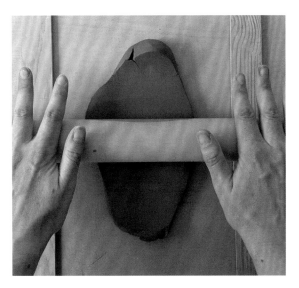

1 There are many ways to make a handle. For this project the handle is cut from a slab. Roll out some clay to a thickness of around 1.25cm (½in). Using a straight edge and a potter's knife, cut a strip of clay around 2cm (¾in) wide.

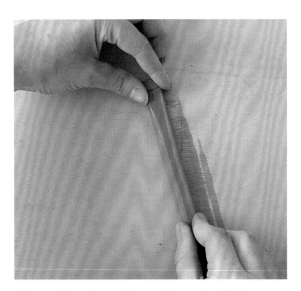

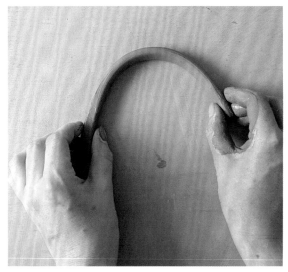

2 Smooth the edges with a wet finger, then lift the handle at one end and smooth the shape.

3 Lay the handle back down on your workbench on its side in a curve and leave to firm up. You can firm it up more quickly with a heat gun.

4 To attach the handle, cut the clay to approximately the right length. Hold it against the mug and when you're happy, mark its position.

5 Using a comb, score and then slip your marked points and firmly press on the handle.

6 To make sure the handle is firmly attached, extrude a small piece of clay and fix that around the joint, smoothing into place with a modelling tool.

7 Dry your piece slowly to prevent the handle joint from cracking. I tend to wrap mine in plastic for a day or two to keep the piece damp. Once it's bisque fired you can sand off any burrs.

FINISHES

For this project, I have inlaid a gloss white glaze into the combed grooves. The curve at the base is left unglazed, so paint a layer of wax around the bottom portion as well as on the base of the mug, then leave to dry.

The whole of the mug is going to be covered in a gloss white, so the easiest way to achieve this is dipping it into your bucket of glaze using a pair of tongs and then pouring out the glaze. Using tongs prevents there being any finger marks.*

Once the glaze has dried, handling it very carefully, use a flexible metal kidney-shaped rib to scrape the surface, leaving the glaze just in the grooves and around the lip.

A rib with a pointed end is helpful here to cut a sharp line around the lip. Use a turning tool to scrape the glaze away from under the handle.

*NOTE: On some pieces, I like to include the finger marks (for example, the Fluted Stem Vase on pages 60–65) as it adds to the handmade quality of the vessel. However, for this project I'm concentrating on achieving a very crisp, neat look, so I don't want finger marks to interrupt the lines.

Contrast-Carved Planter

The technique of pinching clay to form a vessel is the oldest form of pottery. There is something extremely therapeutic about this way of working. It's a slow process – much slower than the potter's wheel – but the advantage is that it allows you to really understand clay as a material, how it behaves and how best to handle it.

CLAY

Approx. 1kg
(2lb) of finely
grogged black
stoneware

TOOLS AND
MATERIALS

For Forming
Banding wheel
Surform
Sponge

For Carving
Loop tool
Liquid latex
Flexible metal
  kidney-shaped rib

FIRING

Bisque fired to cone
06 and glaze fired
to cone 6 in an
electric kiln

The clay I've used for this project is a grogged black stoneware. With the intentionally imperfect shape and the maker's marks that are left by the pinching technique, I think it adds a timeless feel to the piece. I've gone for a finely grogged clay rather than a coarse grog. This gives the texture I'm after but doesn't get in the way of the carving. If the clay is too heavily grogged, it would interfere with the pattern and be difficult to carve.

The carving on this planter is a simple overlapping pattern made with a loop tool. The striking effect of this piece comes from the contrast of textures – the rough, earthy black clay and the smooth gloss of the white glaze highlighted by the carved design.

I love the contrast of the white glaze on the black clay – it really makes the design stand out. You can experiment with different carved designs on your planter, revealing just a little of the black clay underneath will give the same striking effect.

FORMING

This project is for a planter approximately 18cm (7in) in diameter.

1 We're going to make a basic pinch pot for this project. Holding your ball of clay in one hand, push the thumb of your other hand into the centre. Keep pushing your thumb downwards until you start to feel it in your supporting hand. That lets you know that your base is the right thickness.

2 Moving in a circle, gently widen the base by squeezing with your thumb and fingers. When you have your base to the desired width, set your pot onto your banding wheel.

3 Apply consistent pressure between the thumb and fingers of one hand as you gradually work your way around the pot, turning the banding wheel slowly with the other hand. Start from the base and spiral your way up to the top. Using the tip of your thumb on the inside of the pot will help to stop it flaring out too much.

NOTE: You may need to allow the clay to firm up a little halfway through. We're using a grogged clay here, which has a very firm structure, ideal for hand-building. However, if you find your clay is becoming too soft to work with, leave it for half an hour and come back to it; you'll then be able to thin the walls more easily without risking the pot collapsing.

4 Once leather-hard, you can use a surform (a tool a bit like a small cheese grater) to refine the curve at the base of the pot. With a pinch pot you'll find that you'll end up with a wobbly rim. You can trim this off to get a perfectly even top, however, I prefer to leave it with its natural wobble; I think it adds to its hand-built character.

5 To finish, gently smooth over the pot with a damp sponge, but make sure you don't erase all of your fingermarks as they also contribute to the character of the piece.

CARVING

This project has a more rustic feel than those thrown on the potter's wheel, so I don't like to measure out too much or try to make the carving too even – I prefer it to have a more spontaneous feel but this of course is up to you.

1 Starting from just below the rim of the pot, use the rounded end of your loop tool to carve out a small piece of clay. Work your way around the rim, following the undulating line and lifting the tool off gently at the end of each stroke to get a smooth, oval shape.

2 The second row of carving overlaps the first slightly and is placed in between the grooves.

3 Repeat to create a third row.

4 Give everything a sponge over to smooth any harsh lines and give the carving a subtle feel.

FINISHES

The bottom section of this planter has been left unglazed. The raw clay has such a tactile, rough texture that I like to leave a portion of it exposed. For the rest of the pot I've used a simple gloss white glaze.

I use a liquid latex to cover the parts of the pot that I want to leave as raw clay. I find latex works better than wax on a grogged clay like this one as it gets into all the tiny crevices.

1. Apply the liquid latex to the bottom portion and base of the pot, following the curves of your carving.

2. Once the latex is dry, dip your pot into your white glaze. Leave for a few minutes until the glaze has dried then peel off the latex. Note – always wear a mask when dealing with dry glaze.

3. To highlight the carved design, use the edge of a flexible metal kidney-shaped rib to scrape the glaze from just the surface of the carved section.

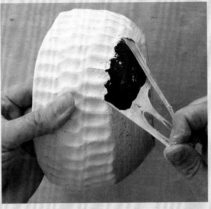

Fluted Stem Vase

This is a really simple technique and one of the first that I tried when I started out in ceramics. As with all carving techniques, the state of the clay is paramount; too soft and the shape of the pot will warp as you press into it; too firm and the tool will scratch through the clay rather than cutting through it smoothly. It takes a bit of practice to get to know when it's just right; experiment a little and you'll soon find the sweet spot.

CLAY

Approx. 1kg
(2lb) of buff
stoneware

TOOLS AND MATERIALS

For Forming
Throwing rib
Sponge or chamois
   leather
Sponge on a stick
Turning tool

For Fluting
Banding wheel
Marking tool
Loop tool
Sponge

FIRING

Bisque fired to cone
06 and glaze fired
to cone 6 in an
electric kiln

The narrow neck on this vase makes it great for holding single stems of flowers and I often fill it with whatever is in bloom in my garden. They work well in a collection of different sizes and it's an easy way to create a stylish display with only a few flowers!

I've used a round-ended loop tool on this project but there are lots of different shapes and sizes available. A straight-ended tool will carve squared-off corners at the top of the vase, giving a slightly different look, and you can experiment with different widths of fluting depending on the size of your tool (see below).

These vases are simple to make and look fantastic grouped together like this. Why not make a few in varying heights and widths united by a simple but effective fluted design.

FORMING

This project is for a small vase with a narrow neck, approximately 13cm (5in) tall.

1 Start by coning and centring the clay on your wheel.

2 Use your thumbs to drill a hole in the centre, then open up the base to the desired width.

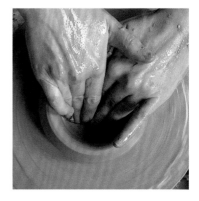

3 Use your fingers or a sponge to compress the base. This will help to prevent the base from cracking later on.

4 Start pulling up the walls. Apply more pressure on the outer wall to keep the form from flaring out. Make sure to leave a little extra thickness in the walls to allow for the carving.

5 Once your piece is at the desired height, straighten up the walls with your rib tool. I like my vases to have a slightly tapered shape.

6 Before you narrow the neck, make sure you take the water out of the bottom of the vessel with a sponge on a stick.

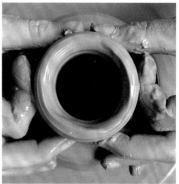

8 To define the shape, use both thumbs, both knuckles of your first fingers and both middle fingers to narrow the neck further. Having many points of contact on this delicate part of the vessel helps to prevent the clay from rippling as you compress it.

7 To narrow the lip, gently compress the clay a couple of inches from the top of the vase, moving your hands up the vessel as you go. Take two or three gentle strokes to encourage the clay in and to prevent it from rippling.

9 Now that you've compressed the clay, you'll have a little extra to work with, so pull up the top of the lip. I like to give mine a flared shape but experiment with your own design.

10 Smooth the lip with a sponge or piece of chamois leather then leave to firm up until leather-hard.

TRIMMING

1 To trim a piece with a narrow rim like this one it's easiest to use a chuck as a support. Throw a low, thick cylinder that will hold your leather-hard vase upside down, keeping the delicate rim off the wheel head. Get rid of any excess water and slip using a sponge.

2 With clean, dry hands place your vase upside down in the chuck. Make sure that it's centred and then press down firmly to secure it.

3 Keep a finger on the centre of the base to keep it steady and use your turning tool to get rid of any excess clay on the bottom.

CARVING

around the pot using firm, steady strokes with your loop tool. One decisive stroke will have a crisper look than going over it several times, so be confident! As you carve the last few strokes, keep an eye on the space left to fill. You can alter the width of your flutes marginally to make sure you're not left with an odd gap at the end.

1 While your vase is still leather-hard, you can create your carved design. Place your pot on a banding wheel and lightly mark a horizontal line where you want your fluting to start.

2 Make sure you can hold your vase comfortably; resting it on a piece of foam or fabric can work well but for a small vase like this I find I have most control over it by holding it in my hand as I carve. Work your way

FINISHES

I really like the clay to shine through with this technique, so I always use a very simple glaze, in this case a translucent matt white. It gives a hint of the soft speckle and earthy colour of the buff stoneware beneath and adds to the tactile quality of the piece.

3 Sponge over the whole design to smooth any rough edges and get rid of your guidelines.

4 Once bisque fired, gently sand the piece to get rid of any burrs.

Incised Candle Holder

Instead of using carving to add to the surface of the piece, with this project we're cutting right through the clay to create our design. This vessel is perfect as a candle holder, as it projects the pattern around the room when the candle is lit, creating a really cosy feel.

CLAY

Approx. 1.4kg
(3lb) of buff
stoneware

TOOLS AND
MATERIALS

For Forming
Throwing rib
Sponge
Chamois leather
Pointed turning tool
Potter's wire
Turning tool

For Incising
Small work board
Banding wheel
Set square
Marking tool
Potter's knife
Pipe cleaner
Sponge
Potter's needle

FIRING

Bisque fired to cone
06 and glaze fired
to cone 6 in an
electric kiln

With this project, not all the cuts are exactly the same thickness or precisely parallel. The imperfections add character; something you don't get with a mass-produced factory piece! So don't worry if your lines are a little crooked – embrace it!

Removing so much of the wall of the pot does mean that it is a lot more fragile while it's drying than some of the other projects. I would recommend placing your pot on a small work board before you begin carving. That way you can move the pot when you've finished without damaging it. Try to handle it as little as possible while it's drying.

You could experiment with a few different designs and patterns as below. I used a hole cutter for the circular pattern. A small sponge on a stick is useful for smoothing off the edges of the larger cut-outs.

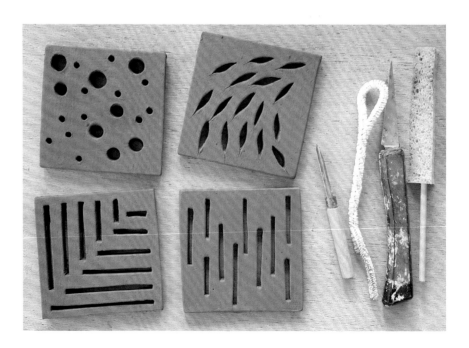

The key thing to remember with this project is that you want to remove enough clay so that the light can shine through and create that cosy candlelit feel, but not so much that the structural integrity of your piece is compromised.

FORMING

This project is for a candle holder approximately 13cm (5in) tall.

1 Start by coning and centring the clay on the wheel.

2 Use your thumbs to drill a hole in the centre, then open up the base. I've given mine a fairly wide base so that it will be able to comfortably fit a large candle.

3 Use your fingers or a sponge to compress the base. This will help to prevent the base from cracking later on.

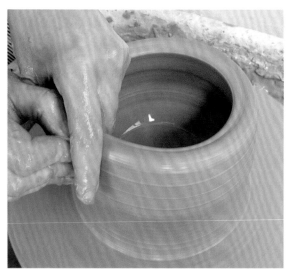

4 Start pulling up the walls. Apply more pressure on the outer wall to keep the form from flaring out.

5 Once your piece has reached the desired height, you can straighten up the walls with your rib tool. I like this piece to have an ever-so-slightly tapered shape.

6 To create the small lip at the top, gently compress the clay at the top of the pot inwards with your hands, then guide the lip upwards. I've left a wide opening at the top to make it easier to get a candle in and out and to be able to light it safely.

7 Smooth the lip with a sponge or piece of chamois leather, cut in a notch at the base with a pointed turning tool, run a wire under the base then leave to firm up.

Once leather-hard, secure the pot upside down on your wheel and use a turning tool to trim off any excess clay and cut in a chamfered edge.

CARVING

While your vase is still leather-hard, you can create your carved design. There's a careful balance between the pot being pliable enough for you to be able to cut through it easily, while being firm enough to hold its shape while you remove sections of the walls. You'll also find that if the clay is too wet the cut-away pieces of clay will stick as you try to remove them, making it more difficult to get a clean finish. The best way to learn when it is in the perfect state is just trial and error. Start when it's slightly on the softer side and see how the clay behaves. If it's sticking or begins to sag, leave it for an hour or two then come back to it and try again. You'll quickly learn to know when it's ready just by how the clay feels to the touch.

1 Place your piece on a small work board then onto your banding wheel. I want the design to look hand-carved and not too precise, but it still needs to flow around the piece: I don't want to end up getting all the way round the pot and finding my design doesn't line up. To give yourself a rough guideline to work with, use a set square and a soft marking tool (I find a rubber-tipped tool works well) to draw a series of vertical lines around the pot. Turning the banding wheel with one hand and, holding the marking tool steady in the other hand, draw a few horizontal lines to give you a rough grid to work from.

2 Carve out your design. Keep one hand inside the pot to (very carefully!) feel that the tip of the knife has come right through the wall. Having two hands controlling the knife also helps to keep the line steady.

3 Taking your time, work your way around the pot. Sometimes I find that the top of the pot is ready to carve before the bottom as it tends to dry more quickly. In this case, I would carve the top portion then leave it to firm up a little more before carving the bottom section.

4 To smooth off the sharp edges, you need to get in between each of the incised lines. I've experimented with a few different tools and I've found for these really small cuts, a pipe cleaner tends to work best. Keep a bowl of water beside you and, keeping the pipe cleaner damp, work your way around the pot. It's a pretty time-consuming process but it makes all the difference in giving your candle holder a beautiful finish.

5 Lastly, gently smooth over the entire pot with a sponge; making sure you erase all the lines from your marked grid.

FINISHES

I love the gloss finish of this white glaze; it breaks slightly on the carved edges revealing the speckles in the clay underneath and it reflects the candlelight beautifully when it's lit. After you've dipped your candle holder in your glaze, use a potter's needle to get rid of any lumps of glaze that have caught in the incisions.

Faceted Jug

This has got to be one of the most satisfying carving techniques; the feeling of slicing through the clay and even the sound as it draws through the pot! As always, to get a great finish you need your clay to be in just the right state; try and catch it when it's on the soft side of leather-hard. When you draw your tool through the clay to cut your facets, it should glide smoothly and cut a sharp line.

CLAY

Approx. 1.8kg
(4lb) of a mixture
of buff and flecked
stoneware

TOOLS AND MATERIALS

For Forming
Straight wooden rib
Sponge on a stick
Small-tipped
  modelling tool
Scoring tool
Slip

For Faceting
Cheese slice
Turning tools

FIRING

Bisque fired to cone
06 and glaze fired
to cone 6 in an
electric kiln

Faceting is a simple technique to master, as the central bar of the cheese slice stops you from cutting into the clay too deeply. Just make sure that you pull your walls up evenly and leave a bit of extra thickness when you throw your pot.

I've used a flat wire, but you can experiment with pottery 'wiggle wires' which can give some great effects (see below). You can change the direction of the wire as you draw it down the pot, creating a zigzag effect or use a sweeping movement to create a more organic feel.

The simplicity of this technique allows you to create some really sharp, precise and striking designs, perfectly combining style and functionality.

FORMING

This project is for a tapered jug approximately 25cm (10in) tall.

To create the speckle in this piece, I have used a mixture of two different clays: a buff stoneware and a flecked stoneware. I wanted a subtle speckle so have used 20% flecked and 80% buff but you can experiment to get a look that you like.

1 Wedge your clays together to get them really well mixed.

2 Cone and centre the clay, then use your thumbs to drill a hole in the centre and open up the base, keeping it fairly narrow.

3 Start pulling up the walls. Apply more pressure on the outer wall to keep the form from flaring out.

4 If your piece starts to flare out, collar it back in by gripping both hands gently around the base of the pot. Stroke upwards, applying more pressure as you move up the vessel.

5 Make sure to leave some extra thickness in the walls to allow for the faceting.

6 Smooth and straighten the walls with your throwing rib and remove any water from inside the jug with your sponge on a stick.

CARVING

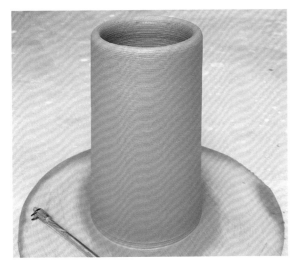

1 Leave your jug to firm up ever so slightly. You want to be able to carve through it easily but it still needs to be pliable enough to form the lip. Normally you would form the lip straight after throwing but for this project I want the carving to cover the whole piece so I form the lip after faceting.

2 Holding the cheese slice with two hands, start at the top and smoothly but confidently draw your tool down to the bottom. Repeat around the vessel – I find it easiest to place the pot on the wheel for this.

You'll know if the clay is in the correct state as it'll cut smoothly without sticking or burring at the edges.

3 To tidy up the bottom and give an elegant shape to the jug, place it upside down on the wheel head and use your turning tools to create a lovely curve.

ALTERNATIVE TOOL

For a different look, try a wiggle wire. With the same technique, it creates a very different effect. You can either draw the tool down the pot in straight lines to create grooves or, as I've done here, move the wire from side to side.

FORMING THE LIP

When positioning the lip, think about where your handle will be. The two will need to be opposite each other, so form your lip opposite the flat edge of a facet to give you room to place the handle.

1 To form the lip, wet the clay slightly. Using your thumb and middle finger stroke the clay upwards to thin it a little.

2 Create a 'V' shape with the first two fingers of your left hand (this will support the shape of the lip), then use the index finger of your right hand to gently stroke the clay down in between your two fingers to form the lip.

ATTACHING THE HANDLE

1 Holding a lump of clay in one hand, gently but firmly draw the clay down. Keep your hand wet to allow the clay to slide smoothly and repeat the action until the clay thins and lengthens. Pull the handle longer than you need then lay it down on your workbench, cutting it from the lump.

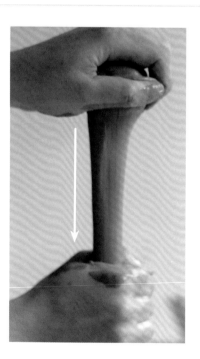

2 When it's firmed up a little, turn it onto its side and create the curve.

3 To attach the handle to the jug, cut the handle to approximately the right length. Hold it up against the jug and, when you're happy, mark its position.

4 Score and slip your marked points and firmly press on the handle.

5 To make sure the handle is firmly attached, extrude a small piece of clay and fix that around the joint, smoothing into placing with a modelling tool.

6 Dry your piece slowly to prevent the handle joint cracking. I tend to wrap mine in plastic for a day or two to keep the piece damp.

FINISHES

I've used a simple white gloss glaze on this project. It allows the larger iron particles in the flecked stoneware to burn through giving a lovely speckle, while still feeling subtle with a simple, rustic feel.

Impressed Mini Planter

This project is a slightly different take on carving. Instead of carving the clay itself, we're going to carve into linoleum, impress this design into a slab of clay then form into a vessel. Make sure your clay is nice and soft as it will pick up the details of the pattern more easily.

CLAY

Approx. 1kg
(2lb) of soft buff
stoneware

TOOLS AND
MATERIALS

For Forming
Craft linoleum
Metal rule
Scalpel
Set square
Lino-cutting tool
Canvas
Rolling pin
Rolling guides
Rubber kidney-
  shaped rib
Corn starch
Lino roller
Potter's knife
Cylindrical form
  such as a rigid
  cardboard tube
Comb for scoring
Slip
Modelling tool
Work board
Marking tool
Surform
Banding wheel
Turning tool
Sponge

FIRING

Bisque fired to cone
06 and glaze fired
to cone 6 in an
electric kiln

There are limitless options for design here. I tend to favour quite simple, geometric patterns but you could do absolutely anything you liked. Perhaps have a play around on some small squares of linoleum and create some test tiles (see below). Once you've carved into the linoleum, there's no undoing it, so creating test tiles is the perfect way to make sure you're happy with your design before you begin the real thing.

I've used a really simple shape for this planter but you could adjust the dimensions to make lots of different vessels; a tall vase perhaps. Or even add a handle and turn it into a mug.

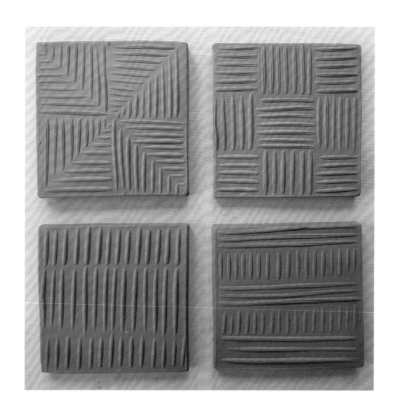

Once you've mastered this technique, you can apply it to absolutely any vessel and with any design you like. And once you've created your pattern on linoleum, you can reuse it again and again to make a series of pieces.

FORMING

This project is for a small planter, approximately 6cm (2¼in) tall.

1 Using a scalpel and metal rule, cut your linoleum to the same size as the slab of clay you'll need to construct your pot. For this planter, my linoleum was 38 x 10cm (15 x 4in) but it will depend on the size of the form you are creating.

Give yourself a rough guide to work from by marking out your design in pencil. Use a set square to make sure your lines are parallel. Carve your pattern with your lino tool. The tool I used here has a small scooped blade. Keep your hands away from the blade and always carve away from you.

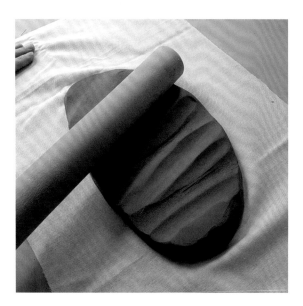

2 Place your clay onto a piece of canvas (this will make it easier to manoeuvre later on) and give it a good bash with your rolling pin. This will thin it out a little and mean there's less rolling to do.

3 Using your rolling guides, roll the clay to a thickness of around 5mm (¼in). Turn the clay over once or twice as you roll it and roll it all directions to help prevent warping.

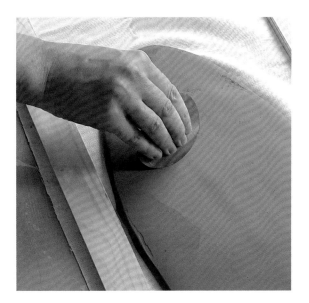

4 Smooth over the slab with a rubber kidney-shaped rib to give an even surface for your pattern.

5 Linoleum has a tendency to stick to damp clay so, to prevent this, sprinkle some corn starch then brush it over the clay to form a thin layer. This will soak up any surface moisture and will burn off in the kiln later on.

6 Lay your linoleum, pattern side down, onto your slab. Use your lino roller to press the linoleum into the clay. Be quite firm with it; you want to impress all the details of your pattern.

7 Cut around your piece of linoleum with the potter's knife and discard the excess clay.

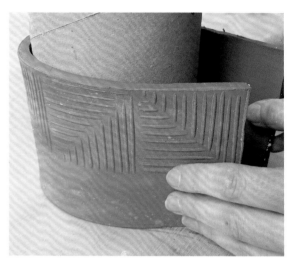

8 Carefully peel back the linoleum from the clay and leave to firm up a little. You want the clay to be supple enough so that you can manoeuvre it without it stretching or becoming misshapen but still pliable enough to be wrapped around your form without cracking.

9 Take your slab of clay and carefully wrap it around your form. Here, I've used an old cardboard tube.

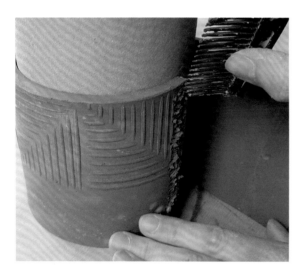

10 Where the clay overlaps, score some lines with a comb and apply some slip, then firmly press together. The corn starch will have soaked up some of the surface moisture, so make sure you use a good amount of slip to make the join really strong. Use your modelling tool and a wet finger to smooth over the joins. You could cut the overlap so the join is invisible but I prefer to leave it visible; I like that it shows how the pot was made. Carefully set this part aside, leaving the form in place.

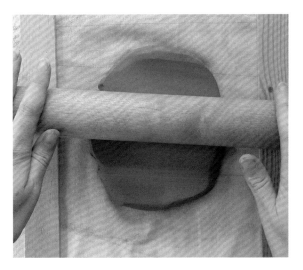

11 Roll out a small piece of clay onto a piece of canvas on a work board. This will form the base of your planter.

12 Gently place the walls of your pot onto the base then draw around it with a marking tool.

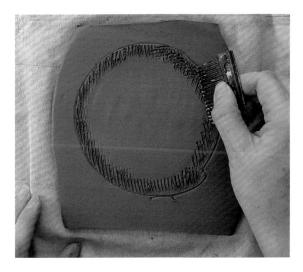

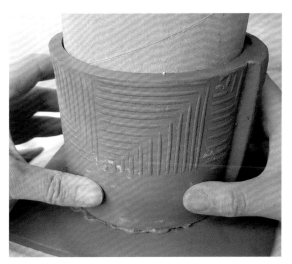

13 Remove your pot, then score and apply slip inside your marked line.

14 Place the walls back onto the base and gently press down to attach.

15 Carefully cut the base to size. Try to keep the blade as upright as possible to create a seamless line from the walls down to the base.

16 Use a modelling tool and a wet finger to smooth the joins. You can remove the form at this point to get to the inside and smooth the joins here as well.

17 When your pot is leather-hard, you can tidy up the shape a little, if necessary. I use a surform to get rid of any lumps and bumps, particularly where the walls of the pot meet the base. The surform shaves off tiny pieces of clay and can be smoothed over afterwards with a sponge.

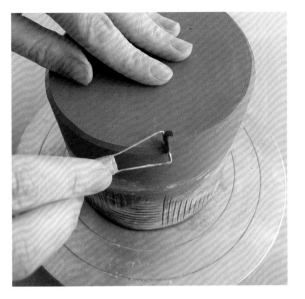

18 I always cut a chamfered edge into the bottom of my pots. It creates a shadow gap which I think adds a bit of elegance to a piece, as it makes it appear as if it floats and it also creates a line to apply your glaze up to. On a hand-built pot like this one, it's easy to do by placing the pot upside down on your banding wheel, turning the wheel with one hand, while trimming the edge at an angle with a turning tool.

19 Lastly, run a sponge over the rim to soften the edge.

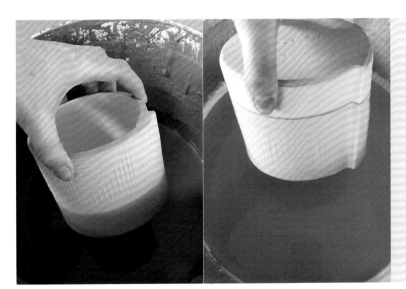

FINISHES

This combination of a black and white glaze is one that I use a lot in my work. I love the soft, mottled grey that's created where the two glazes overlap. I apply the glazes so that the impressed pattern is covered by just the matt white. This glaze is translucent and breaks very subtly over the raised pattern.

Sgraffito Serving Plate

Aesthetically, I love the simple yet striking design of this piece and I find the carving of tiny lines between concentric circles to be quite a meditative process. This plate works well as a functional piece but would also look great as a decorative item hung on the wall or propped on a shelf.

CLAY

Approx. 1.8kg
(4lb) of smooth white
stoneware

TOOLS AND MATERIALS

For Forming
Sponge
Curved wooden rib
Rubber kidney-
  shaped rib
Chamois leather
Potter's wire
Turning tool

For Sgraffito
Coloured slip
Flat brush
Sgraffito tool
Soft brush
Sandpaper

FIRING

Bisque fired to cone
06 and glaze fired
to cone 6 in an
electric kiln

I've used a royal blue slip here which gives a great contrast to the white clay that's revealed as you scratch through it. I make my slip using a body stain and for this level of vibrancy I have used a 15% ratio of stain to powdered clay.

The clay for this project is a very smooth, white stoneware. For fine sgraffito work like this, I find a smooth clay works better than a grogged body as it allows you to easily cut a clean line through the slip.

By using a bold-coloured slip and a simple repeating design, you can create a really impressive and intricate-looking piece.

FORMING

This project is for a serving plate with a diameter of approximately 25cm (10in).

1 Start by coning and centring your clay. Once centred, push your clay down into a wide disc. Make sure you leave plenty of clay in the base to form a foot-ring later on.

2 Using your sponge, draw the clay slowly out to the edges of the wheel head.

3 Using your sponge again, lift the edge of the clay to form the rim of your plate.

4 To get an even curve on the inside edge I suggest using a wooden rib. Gently press this into the rim, supporting the outside of the plate with your other hand.

5 Smooth the base of your plate with the rubber kidney-shaped rib. Compressing the clay like this will help to prevent cracking further down the line.

6 Smooth the lip with your sponge or a piece of chamois leather and then carefully wire your plate off the bat of your wheel head.

APPLYING THE SLIP

Leave your plate to firm up slightly before applying the slip. It needs to be no longer tacky to the touch.

Your slip needs to be roughly the consistency of double cream; add a little water and mix well if it's too thick.

1 A flat brush works really well for applying slip, as it can hold a lot of liquid. Load up your brush then, starting from the centre, with the wheel turning, gently draw the brush out to the edge of the plate.

Allow to dry a little before applying a second coat. Once the plate is dry enough to be released from the bat, you can turn it upside down to trim it.

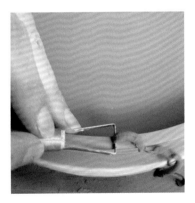

2 Centre the plate on the wheel head and secure it. I simply dampen the wheel head a little and that holds the plate in place. Trim away any excess clay from the base and cut in your foot ring. Carving two foot rings and leaving a small amount of clay right in the very centre will prevent the plate from sagging in the kiln.

3 With the plate the right way up, use your turning tool to remove the slip on the top edge of the rim, creating a neat line as well as removing any slip that has accidentally been painted over the outside of the rim.

CARVING

1 With the wheel spinning at a decent speed, use your sgraffito tool to mark concentric circles. A slip-up here isn't easily fixed, so make sure you're in a comfortable position, use both hands to hold your tool steady and take your time! The wheel is doing the work for you, so choose your point and keep as still as you can.

2 Next, using the same tool, fill in your smaller lines. Don't worry about getting them perfectly straight and evenly spaced; the piece has a nicer quality when the lines are clearly hand-drawn rather than perfectly even.

3 Remove the carved pieces with a soft brush. Don't use a damp sponge as this will smudge your sharp lines.

4 Allow to dry slowly.

5 Once bisque fired, sand the plate lightly to remove any burrs caused by the carving.

6 Apply your chosen glaze.

FINISHES

I've used a simple matt transparent glaze on this plate to let the sgraffito design stand out. I find it easier to brush the glaze on for this type of piece rather than dipping as I can make sure the glaze has filled all the grooves.

Fettled Hanging Planter

I love to fill my home with plants and I'm always looking for interesting ways to display them. Hanging planters are a great way to show off a beautiful trailing plant and hanging it at eye level ensures you can fully appreciate the carved design that covers the whole vessel. The stoneware clay that you'll be using is extremely durable, so this planter could even be used outside.

CLAY

Approx. 1.4kg
(3lb) of buff
stoneware

TOOLS AND
MATERIALS

For Forming
Curved wooden rib
Sponge
Turning tool
Flexible metal
  kidney-shaped rib

For Fettling
Protractor
Hole cutter
Fettling knife

FIRING

Bisque fired to cone
06 and glaze fired
to cone 6 in an
electric kiln

The trick to this technique is keeping the walls of the bowl fairly thick so that when you cut across the curve with your fettling knife, you don't carve right through the wall. It also helps to throw the bowl with a good thick base; this will enable you to get a beautifully rounded shape when you come to trim it. Make sure that your clay is leather-hard before you start carving; if the fettled pieces stick to the bowl as you cut them off, it's too wet. They should peel away easily leaving a clean, sharp line.

For my planter, I've cut away quite large sections of clay, but you could cut much smaller pieces to create a more intricate design (below left), or use a wiggle wire to cut away ridged portions of clay for a completely different look (below right).

This is a really versatile project. As a planter, you can alter the size and vary the design to make it suitable for any home or garden. Or omit the holes for hanging and give it a flat bottom to create a striking bowl.

FORMING

This project is for a planter approximately 20cm (8in) in diameter.

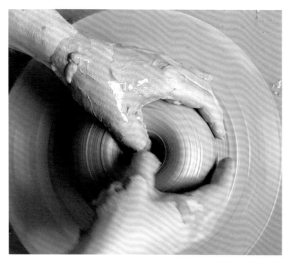

1 Centre your clay on your wheel then drill down to form the base. The base needs to be left quite thick for this project as we're going to trim a considerable amount of clay off to give the rounded shape.

2 Open out the base and start to pull up your walls.

3 You can let the bowl flare out naturally as you raise the walls. Remember to leave plenty of thickness in the walls to allow for the fettling later on.

4 To refine the curve, use a curved wooden rib on the inside while supporting with your other hand on the outside. Start from the base and slowly work your way up to the rim.

5 Take any water out of the base of the bowl with your sponge and smooth the rim.

6 When your bowl is leather-hard, remove the excess clay and refine the shape. Dampen your wheel head to fix the bowl in place upside down. Using your turning tool, start to trim off the edges.

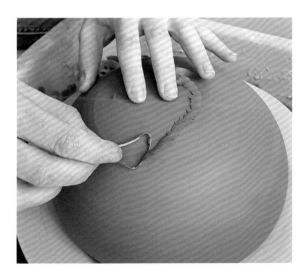

7 Gradually round off the shape until you're left with a half sphere. Take your time; it's easier to take off small amounts bit by bit than trying to remove too much at once.

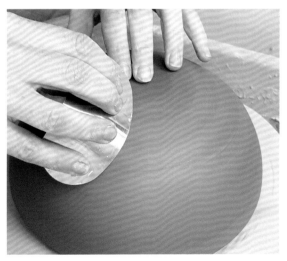

8 Finally, to smooth off the shape, run a flexible steel kidney-shaped rib over the surface. This will give you a great surface for carving.

CARVING

To carve this planter, I find a long-bladed fettling knife works best. The blade is long enough to grip both ends easily, giving you plenty of control when carving.

1 Before we start carving, we're going to cut the holes to allow the planter to be hung.

Place your bowl upside down and, using a protractor, mark three points at 120 degrees around the bowl. Then, use a hole cutter to carve out the holes and smooth over with your sponge.

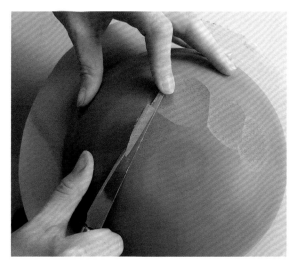
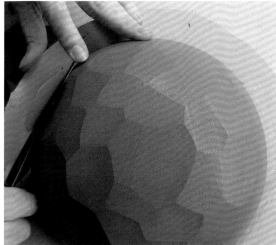

2 Place the bowl upside down to begin carving. The trick here is to get your angle just right. Plenty of times I've carved just a little too deeply and gone right through the wall, so keep your angle shallow. Think about just carving across the top of the curve rather than into the bowl. I like to start from the top and work my way down, so get a good grip on your pot and, with a decent amount of pressure, pull the blade toward you.

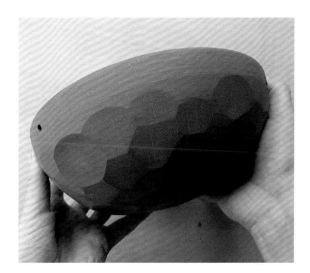

3 Rather than fettling right to the rim, I stop about 2.5cm (1in) from the bottom, leaving a lovely wobbly edge following the line of the cuts.

To finish, thread through some cord or leather, plant it up and enjoy!

FINISHES

I love the look and tactile quality of this clay when left unglazed. On the inside of the planter I've used a soft, matt charcoal which flows over the rim, following the uneven line of the facets and highlighting the design. Note: wax along your carving lines before glazing to get a sharp edge. The wax will burn off in the kiln.

Angle-Carved Candlestick

This is a great project for beginners to the wheel, as you don't need to worry about the thickness of your walls. One of the challenges of carving clay is making sure you don't accidentally carve right through the wall of your piece but for this project you're carving into a solid piece of clay so you can carve as much or as little as you like.

CLAY

Approx. 1.8kg (4lb) of smooth white stoneware

TOOLS AND MATERIALS

For Forming
Metal rule
Straight-edged rib
Chamois leather
Pointed turning tool
Potter's wire

For Angle-Carving
Loop tools (various sizes)
Sharp-tipped turning tool
Potter's wire

FIRING

Bisque fired to cone 06 and glaze fired to cone 6 in an electric kiln

You can either plan out your design on paper before you start or let the design evolve as you go. Either way, take a moment to step back and look at the piece every so often as you're carving to make sure you're happy with the design as it progresses. The candlestick widens towards the base, so I find creating larger angles and leaving wider gaps between the angles as you work toward the base works best aesthetically.

I find it so satisfying to create a design and see it emerge on these candlesticks – when the clay is in just the right state it flies off in paper-thin ribbons as you cut it away.

Perhaps try a different combination of colours and glazes. A gloss white glaze over a black clay (as below) would create an even bolder look.

I've given these elegant candlesticks a modern look by applying glaze over half with a sharp diagonal line. The colour and placement of glaze can dramatically change your design, so don't forget about it during the planning stage.

FORMING

This project is for a candlestick, approximately 25cm (10in) tall.

1 Centre your clay on your wheel by coning it up and then pushing it back down to the wheel head. Do this two or three times then on the final time leave the clay in a cone shape.

2 Now use a gentler movement to refine the shape a little – try to guide the sides into as straight a line as you can. You may find that you need to support the clay with one hand at the top while you do this.

3 To get a neat shape and a sharp line, run a straight-edged tool down the length of your candlestick. I use an old metal rule for this, which works really well.

4 To form the part of the candlestick where the candle will sit, drill down into the top with your finger. It needs to be around 2.5cm (1in) deep to hold a candle securely, allowing for shrinkage when the candlestick dries and is fired.

5 Widen the hole and pull up the walls, then straighten them up with a wooden rib.

6 To get a smooth edge at the top of your candlestick, use a small piece of chamois leather lightly gripped over the top with two fingers.

NOTE: Don't wire your candlestick off the bat once you've finished – we're going to leave it on the bat to carve it. Leave it to dry until it's leather-hard.

CARVING

1 Once leather-hard, you can carve your candlestick. You'll know the clay is in the right state to carve if it cuts away easily in ribbons without sticking. Use the square end of your turning tool, held at an angle, to cut into the clay. Having a variety of different-sized loop tools at hand can be helpful for this stage.

2 I like to carve a variety of different sizes and angles, and leave some portions left uncarved. The key here is to make sure your angles meet perfectly. The sharper the angle, the more successful the overall look will be.

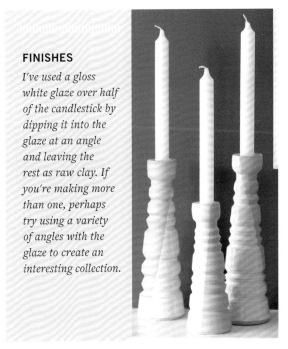

3 When you've finished, use a pointed turning tool to cut a notch at the base to make it easier to wire the candlestick off the bat.

FINISHES

I've used a gloss white glaze over half of the candlestick by dipping it into the glaze at an angle and leaving the rest as raw clay. If you're making more than one, perhaps try using a variety of angles with the glaze to create an interesting collection.

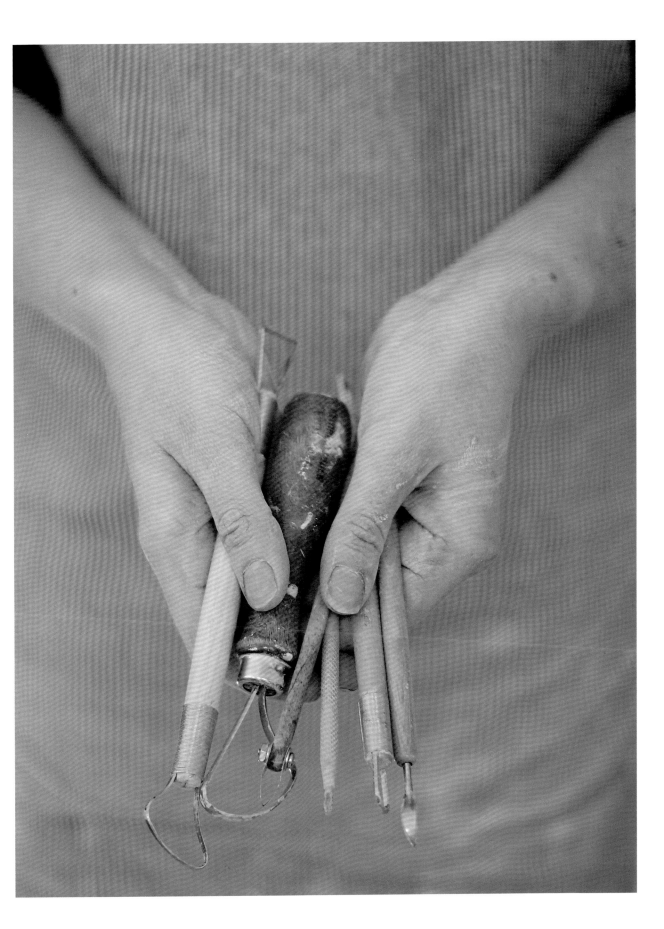

Inlaid Storage Jar

Inlay – or Mishima – is the technique of applying slip into a pattern that has been carved into leather-hard clay. The result is a design that sits flush with the pot giving a very smooth finish.

CLAY

Smooth white stoneware: approx. 700g (1½lb) for the body and 225g (½lb) for the lid

TOOLS AND MATERIALS

For Forming
Throwing rib
Modelling tool
Sponge
Chamois leather
Calipers
Potter's wire
Turning tool
Scoring tool
Slip

For Inlay
Small, pointed loop
  tool
Coloured slip
Slip trailer
Flexible metal
  kidney-shaped rib

FIRING

Bisque fired to cone 06 and glaze fired to cone 6 in an electric kiln

A lidded pot is one of the more complicated forms to make, particularly getting a good fit on the lid. It helps to dry and fire the two parts together and make sure you dry them slowly under plastic to prevent the inlaid slip from cracking away from the body.

There's something magical about scraping away the surface to reveal your design underneath and, as always, there are countless design options here. I tend to use more geometric patterns in my own work and I often make up series of test tiles to experiment with designs (see below).

I've kept my colour scheme simple with just a vibrant royal blue which I think gives a striking contrast to the white clay, but you could use a combination of slip colours for a more intricate design.

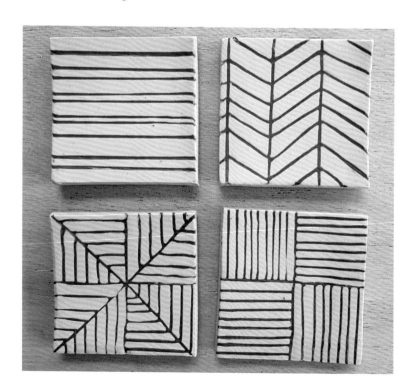

There are endless possibilities for design with this technique. Have fun with some test tiles (see below left) and try out a number of different styles to see what suits you best.

FORMING

This project is for a small storage jar with a lid, measuring 13cm (5in) tall.

When creating lidded vessels, it is important to make the body and the lid together. They will then shrink at the same rate allowing you to get a good fit on your pot.

FORMING THE BODY

1 Start by coning and centring the clay on the wheel.

2 Use your thumbs to drill a hole in the centre then open up the base to the desired width.

3 Start pulling up the walls, applying more pressure on the outer wall to keep the form from flaring out. Leave a little extra thickness in the rim to make the gallery (this is the part that the lid sits on).

4 Once your piece is at the desired height, straighten up the walls using your rib tool.

5 To make the gallery, support either side of the wall and use a flat-ended modelling tool to push the inside edge of the wall down about 1.25cm (½in). If your walls have distorted slightly while making the gallery, gently guide them back into line with your wooden rib.

6 Once you're happy that the walls are free from any lumps and bumps (this will make inlaying the slip later on easier), clean off any water and slip with a sponge and smooth the edges with a chamois leather.

FORMING THE LID

There are lots of different ways to make lids, one of the simplest is to form the lid upside down.

1 Cone and centre your clay then push it down into a flat disc roughly 1.25cm (½in) thick. The disc needs to fit inside the pot and sit on the gallery, so use your calipers to make sure it's roughly the right size. (Don't worry about getting it exact as we'll be able to trim it to the perfect size later on.)

2 To make a flange, push gently out from the centre and lift the clay to form a small wall. Use your calipers to check that this flange will sit within the gallery of the pot.

3 Remove any slip, smooth off the edges and wire it off the bat.

TRIMMING

1 When both the pot and lid have firmed up a little, you can turn the pot upside down and use a turning tool to get rid of any excess clay on the bottom.

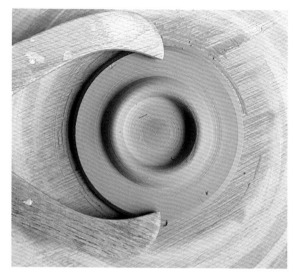

2 Check the fit of your lid using calipers.

3 Trim it, if necessary, to get it just right. You want to leave a little bit of wiggle room here for there to still be a good fit once the piece is glazed.

4 To make sure the top of your lid sits flush with the top of the pot, place the lid on the pot, centre them on the wheel and trim the lid to line up with the rim of the pot. This is an easy way to get a perfect fit.

5 Keeping the pot on the wheel head, you're now going to attach the knob. Score and slip a small area in the centre of the lid and then firmly press down a small ball of clay.

6 With wet fingertips, centre the clay, drill down into the ball of clay and carefully pull up the walls. Create enough height to allow the knob to be gripped easily (approximately 2cm [¾in]) and remember to allow for some shrinkage. Use the chamois leather to smooth the edge of the rim.

CARVING

With your pot and lid still in a leather-hard state, you'll now carve your pattern for the inlay. The pattern I've used for this project involves some horizontal lines, so I find it easiest to carve these on the potter's wheel. (You'll need to dampen your wheel head or fix your pot with small pieces of clay to keep it securely placed.)

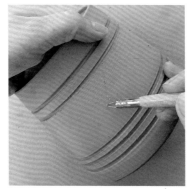

1 With the wheel spinning, use a small loop tool to carve your lines. Place your other hand inside the pot to give support and to make sure you're not carving too deep.

2 The rest of the pattern I carve off the wheel, resting on a piece of foam or fabric to support the pot. I tend to mark out the pattern with a ruler and score it faintly first before carving.

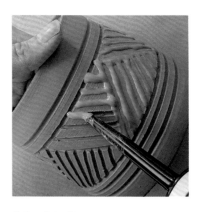

3 The pattern on the lid is made up of concentric circles so carve this on the potter's wheel.

4 Now it is time to fill your carved pattern with a coloured slip. I find it easiest to apply it with a slip trailer. The slip needs to be fairly thick but still able to be smoothly squeezed onto the pot.

5 Carefully fill your carved pattern with a layer of slip. Hold the pot from the inside to avoid smudging.

6 Do the same for the lid.

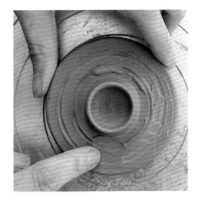

7 The slip needs to fill the grooves completely so after half an hour or so, once the slip has firmed a little, you can push it in with your finger then add a second layer. At this point the slip needs to stand slightly proud of the pot.

8 Leave to dry until the pot is on the firm side of leather-hard then use a metal kidney-shaped rib to scrape away the slip. If your slip is too wet it will smudge, so test a small area first to make sure it's staying put. This is the most satisfying part – the moment when your pattern is revealed!

9 Repeat Steps 7 and 8 for the lid. I find using a turning tool makes it easier to get into those small gaps around the knob. Use some small pieces of clay to help secure the lid to the wheel.

10 Dry your pot and lid slowly to avoid cracking and with the lid in place to maintain a good fit as the pieces shrink.

FINISHES

I've used a matt transparent glaze on this project to give it a smooth surface and allow the pattern to stand out.

Slip-Cast Beaker

Slip-casting is the technique of pouring liquid clay into a plaster mould. It's often used in mass-produced pottery to produce identical pieces or to create forms that can't easily be made on the wheel.

CLAY

1L (1 quart) grey casting slip,
1L (1 quart) white casting slip – depending on the size of your mould (my mould holds around 700ml [¾ quart])

TOOLS AND MATERIALS

For Forming/Slip-Casting
Plaster mould
Measuring jugs
Palette knife or
  other thin blade
Work board
Sponge

For Carving
Marking tool
Banding wheel
Sgraffito scoop tool
Flexible metal
  kidney-shaped rib
Respiratory mask
Brush
Sand paper

FIRING

Bisque fired to cone 06 and glaze fired to cone 6 in an electric kiln

When liquid clay is poured into the mould, the plaster begins to absorb the water, creating a solidifying layer of clay on the inside surface of the mould. After a specified amount of time, the slip is poured out, leaving a deposit of clay in the mould which then stiffens and shrinks and can be removed.

This technique gives us lots of possibilities for carving. In this project we're going to use two colours of casting slip, each poured into the mould and poured out separately, until we build up multiple thin layers of alternating coloured clay. When firm enough to carve, the tool scrapes through the layers to reveal the colours beneath. I've kept to alternating just two colours as I prefer a simple look, but there's no limit to the number of colours you can use. Have a play around and see what you like.

I'm using a plaster mould I made from a thrown cup. If you're making your own mould from a clay piece, remember to consider the shrinkage and always taper the walls outward so that you can get your pot out of your mould.

MAKING COLOURED CASTING SLIP

You can buy coloured casting slips but it's really simple to make your own. You can also tailor your recipe to achieve the exact shade you're after.

For this project I used 28g (1oz) of black body stain to 1 litre (1 quart) of white stoneware casting slip. I added the powdered stain to the slip and blitzed it thoroughly for a few minutes in a kitchen food processor.

Your slip needs to be of a good pouring consistency and free from lumps. Make sure both your grey and your white slips are of the same viscosity. Add a little water if you think it's too thick and mix well but remember that the more water in the mixture, the more it'll shrink.

This technique feels like magic when you carve through the clay to reveal the marbled colours inside. The combination of coloured slips and carved design means you can create truly one-of-a-kind pieces.

FORMING

This project is for a beaker, approximately 8cm (3in) tall.

1 Before you begin, make sure your mould is completely clean and dry and set it on a flat surface.

2 Starting with the grey, pour in the casting slip, filling the mould right to the top and slightly over the rim, as the level of slip in the mould will decrease as the plaster 'drinks' the water. Make sure your jug is able to hold enough slip to fill the mould in one go to avoid a pour line.

3 We want a very thin layer of clay, so wait roughly one minute and then pour the slip back out. Leave the mould upside down to let all the excess clay drip then prop it up at an angle to harden a little. This will prevent you ending up with small drips on the interior base of the beaker. When the slip has lost its sheen it's ready for you to pour the next layer.

4 Now pour in your white slip. Again, pour it right over the rim in one pour.

5 Leave for another minute or so then pour the slip back out, leaving it propped up at an angle.

NOTE: Depending on how many layers you want for your design, repeat steps 2–5; alternating between the grey and white slips. You'll find as you add more layers, the time you'll need to wait before pouring the next layer will increase as the slip will take longer to firm up. For my design I poured seven layers, starting and finishing with the grey slip. Keep a tally of how many layers you've done – it's easy to lose count. And remember that the more layers you add, the thicker the walls of your beaker will be. The exact time required to create the layers will depend on a few factors: the viscosity of your slip, the state of your plaster mould and the air temperature. You'll need to use a little trial and error here to get the timings just right.

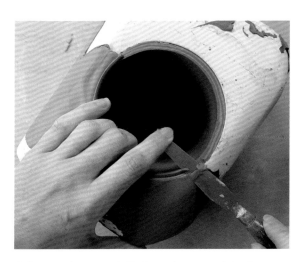

6 Once you've poured all of your layers, wait for the beaker to firm up, then run a palette knife or other flat blade around the top of the mould to cut off the excess. Be careful not to cut into your mould and always pull away from the mould to keep the rim of the beaker as neat as possible.

7 Leave your beaker to firm up until it's leather-hard. (You'll be able to tell the beaker is drying out as it'll come away from the inside of the mould as the slip hardens and shrinks.) I tend to leave mine overnight but it will greatly depend on the temperature and humidity in your studio so check it regularly. To take your beaker out of the mould, place a work board on top and flip it over.

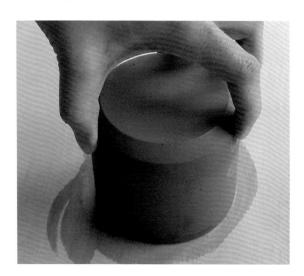

8 To straighten up any unevenness on the rim, dampen a small area on your workbench then, with your beaker upside down, use a gentle, circular motion to rub the rim down slightly.

9 Smooth over the rim gently with a sponge.

CARVING

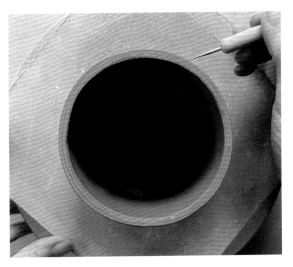

1 Our carving tool for this piece is a sgraffito scoop tool. It has a sharp edge and a shallow curve meaning that all the layers will be visible as we scrape the clay away. Your piece needs to be on the hard side of leather-hard, almost dry, otherwise you'll find the colours of the layers will smudge together.

2 To help keep your lines parallel and even, place your beaker on a banding wheel and use a marking tool to draw a line approximately 1.25cm (½in) below the rim of the cup. Make as light a mark as you can as it will have to be sanded away later.

3 Mark points along this line, roughly 2cm (¾in) apart – these will be the centre points of each carving. Measure the points onto a piece of scrap paper, wrap this around the beaker and use this as a guide for your marks.

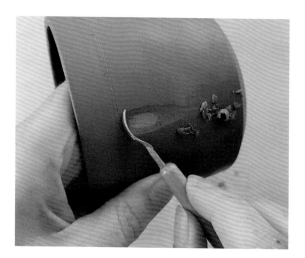

4 Starting from your marking line, confidently stroke your carving tool down the beaker to the bottom. I like to create a teardrop shape, so I apply more pressure at the top of the stroke and ease off as I get to the bottom. With most other carving I would always try to carve the line in one go, however, for this project it needs lots of smaller strokes to gradually reveal the layers. Wear a respiratory mask to prevent you from breathing in the clay dust.

5 Make sure you hold your beaker in a way that feels comfortable to you, as you need to be able to use the tool in a fluid motion. I find the most natural position for me is to support the inside of the pot with the fingers of one hand while I carve with the other. Work your way around the pot, checking as you go that your carved lines are relatively even and vertical.

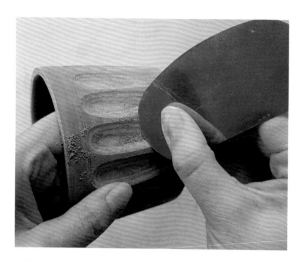

6 Once you've carved all the way around the pot, go over your design gently with your metal kidney-shaped rib. It has a larger curve so will even off your lines and create a neat finish. There is no need to go over multiple times with the rib – it's just for the finishing touch.

7 Brush away any clay dust. We want to keep the layers as defined as possible so avoid using a sponge to smooth over any burrs at this stage.

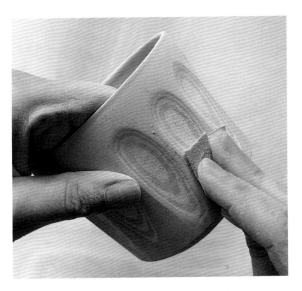

8 Once bisque fired, you can sand away any burrs.

9 Finally, give the piece a wipe over with a damp sponge to clean off any dust.

FINISHES

The only glaze I use on this piece is a transparent gloss on the inside and over the lip. I prefer to leave the majority of the outside as raw clay; I prefer the pattern to be the focus and I don't feel a glaze would add anything here. The clear gloss glaze on the inside and the lip makes it food-safe and more comfortable to drink from. To get a precise parallel line of glaze around the lip of the cup, use a small spirit level; placing it on top of the cup as you dip it into the bucket.

Bellied Bowl

This technique is a much less precise way of carving than some of the other techniques we've looked at as you're letting the wheel do a lot of the work for you.

CLAY

Approx. 1kg
(2lb) of a mixture
of buff and flecked
stoneware (80%
buff, 20% flecked)

TOOLS AND
MATERIALS

For Forming
Straight wooden rib

For Bellying
Small loop tool
Curved wooden rib
Cutting-in tool
Potter's wire
Sponge

FIRING

Bisque fired to cone
06 and glaze fired
to cone 6 in an
electric kiln

The shape of the bowl is made by first throwing a cylinder and carving into it while it's still wet, then pushing out the shape from the inside to form a bowl. The carved design widens and softens and the sweeping curves are exaggerated as the shape is bellied out. The result is a bowl with a beautifully organic quality. It reminds me of the ripples left in the sand when the tide has gone out and I love its raw, natural feel.

You can create a variety of different designs depending on the type of tools you use (see below).

Here, I've used a narrow-ended tool to create a criss-cross pattern. The pattern softens and widens as the bowl flares out.

Here, I've used a much wider-ended tool to cut quite shallow facets. This creates a softer, more subtle look to the piece.

The act of bellying this bowl – forming the shape by pushing the already carved clay from the inside on the wheel – gives a softness that isn't always easy to achieve when carving.

FORMING

This project is for a bowl with a diameter of approximately 9cm (3½in).

1 To make this bowl, start by throwing a thick-walled cylinder. Cone and centre your clay, open up and compress the base then pull up the walls.

2 Pull up the walls to approximately 13cm (5in) high. This is much higher than the finished bowl will be but you will lose a lot of height when you widen your bowl.

3 Try to make the thickness of the walls as even as possible. The bowl will be bellied out from the inside without you touching the outside, so any adjustment in the thickness of the walls needs to be done before carving. A wooden rib works well for this; push the clay from the inside against the straight edge of the rib, slowly working your way up the pot.

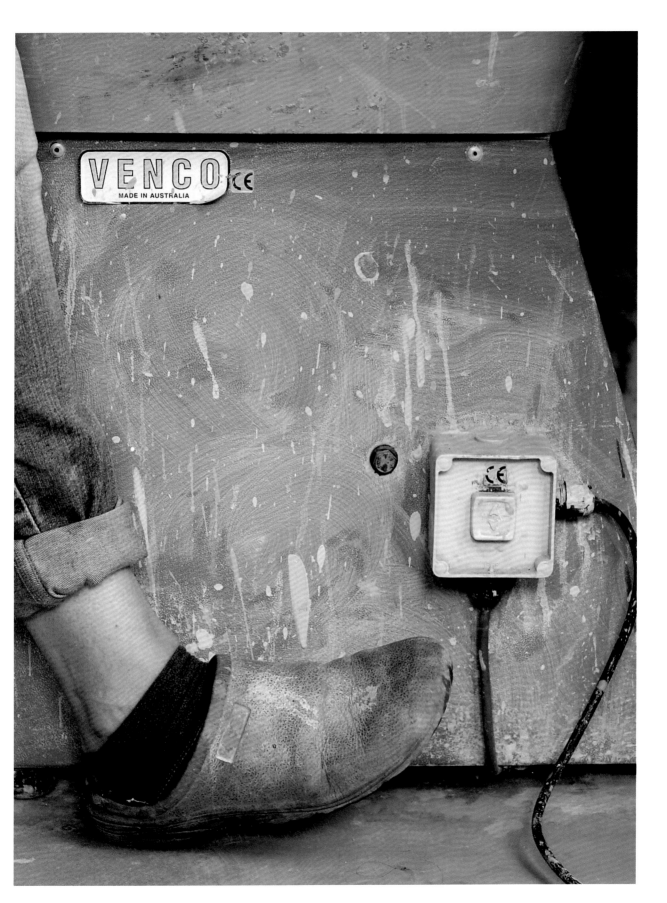

CARVING

1 For this project, I recommend a small, circular loop tool. Keep your pot on the wheel head but not spinning. Start from the bottom and sweep your tool up to the top in a curve. Repeat this all the way around the vessel. My wheel spins anticlockwise, so I carve in the same direction. The turning of the wheel will accentuate this curve when we belly out the shape.

2 The bowl should have an organic quality so don't worry about being perfectly precise or even. Do make sure, however, not to carve too deeply near the rim of the bowl; taper off gently as you finish your strokes. The clay will thin considerably at the rim as we belly it out and if it's too thin it will just tear.

3 Keep the clay wet, particularly the outside. You'll have limited control of the outside of the bowl and this will help it to remain supple. With the wheel spinning, place one hand inside the bowl and push gently outwards, starting from the base and moving up to the rim.

4 Several lighter strokes will be more effective than one or two more forceful ones. You want to gently encourage the clay outwards.

5 Use a curved wooden rib on the inside to refine the shape. Inevitably there'll be some extra thickness at the base. Don't worry about this as we'll trim any excess off when it's leather-hard.

6 Once you're happy with the shape, use your cutting-in tool to make a groove at the base then wire it off the bat.

7 Once it's leather-hard, you can trim off any excess clay and refine the shape. I like to give mine a soft, rounded base with a small foot ring.

8 Finish by sponging over the curves to soften the edges to give it a subtle, natural feel.

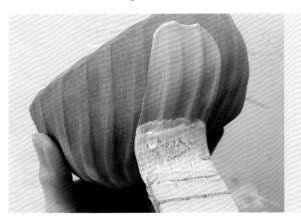

FINISHES

I like the finish to reflect the less refined style of the carving. I've used a pale green slip, which I painted on once the bowl was leather-hard. I then finished the piece with a matt white glaze over the top. This soft glaze allows the natural speckles in the flecked clay to show through.

Agateware Serving Bowl

Agateware is a type of pottery that uses a mixture of coloured clays. The name comes from the marbled effect – which mimics the look of agate stone – that is produced when the mixed clays are thrown on the potter's wheel.

CLAY

Approx. 1.4kg (3lb) of clay – a combination of white stoneware and grey stoneware

TOOLS AND MATERIALS

For Staining Clay
Pestle and mortar
Coloured stain
Respiratory mask
Digital weighing
  scales
Plaster bat

For Forming
Straight-sided
  wooden rib
Sponge or chamois
  leather
Pointed turning tool
Potter's wire
Turning tool
Sand paper

For Agateware
Banding wheel
Various loop tools

FIRING

Bisque fired to cone 06 and glaze fired to cone 6 in an electric kiln

When you carve into a vessel made with marbled clay, an intricate pattern appears where the tool has cut through the various layers of colour. This is such a fun technique – I love carving away the clay to reveal the pattern. You never quite know what you're going to get and every piece is completely unique.

I've used a white stoneware here and stained a portion of it to create a grey clay. You can, of course, buy pre-coloured clay but it is very easy and much less expensive to make your own, and you can adapt the recipe to get just the shade you're after. The percentage of stain that you use will affect the richness of the colour and there is a wide variety of stain colours available for you to experiment with.

The wonderful thing about this technique is that no two bowls will be identical. You're never quite sure what's going to appear until you start carving.

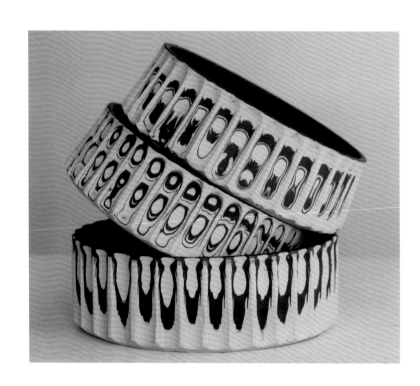

I've gone for a modern, monochromatic look for this serving bowl but there are so many coloured stains to choose from, you could create a really colourful or contrasting look instead.

STAINING THE CLAY

When staining clay for a project like this one, I will usually make a large batch but for these instructions I have given the amounts required specifically to create this bowl.

I want a ratio of 90% white clay to 10% grey. So, for a total of 1.4kg (3lb) of clay, I use 1.26kg (2¾lb) of white stoneware and 140g (5oz) of grey stoneware. Remember to always measure the dry weight to make sure your amounts are accurate.

1 Grind your dry white clay into a rough powder using a pestle and mortar. Always wear a respiratory mask when dealing with dry ingredients.

2 Add your stain to the powdered clay and mix well. (I used a black body stain to achieve a grey colour.)

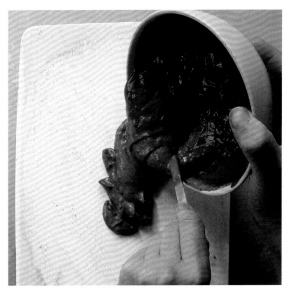

3 Add water to cover and leave it to slake overnight to make sure all the clay particles are broken down.

4 Once all the water has been absorbed, give it a good mix. You want a fairly runny paste. Don't worry if you add too much water; the clay particles will sink to the bottom and you can just tip out any excess water. Tip your stained clay out onto a plaster bat.

5 Leave the clay to firm up for an hour or two (depending on the temperature and humidity of your studio), turning it over halfway through. When it's a workable consistency, wedge the clay to eliminate any air bubbles. It's now ready to use.

FORMING

This project is for a single bowl, approximately 20cm (8in) in diameter.

1 The way in which you position your coloured clays before you start throwing will massively affect the amount of marbling that occurs. I like a defined pattern where the colours don't get too 'muddied.' To achieve this, I don't wedge the two colours together, I cut my ball of white clay (that I've already wedged) in half with a potter's wire and then place my stained clay between the two halves. Then I pat it back into a ball shape making sure I don't trap any air between the layers.

2 Dampen your wheel head slightly then lay on your clay with the stained clay running as a horizontal band through the middle and pat it firmly into place.

3 Usually, when I centre clay on the wheel, I cone the clay up and down several times. If I were to do that with this piece, I would mix my coloured clays too much and lose the defined pattern that I'm after. Therefore, I just cone the clay once then, to make sure it's completely centred, placing the side of my right hand on top and using the heel of my left hand, I push the clay into the middle.

4 Apply more pressure with your right hand, pushing down to shape the clay into a low flat disc.

5 Open the centre of your bowl to form the base then compress it firmly with your sponge – this will help to prevent cracks forming as the piece dries.

6 When your bowl is the desired width, you can start to pull up the walls. Keep them tapered in slightly at this stage. It's easy to angle the walls out later but much more difficult to bring them in again if it flares out too far.

7 Straighten up your walls with your wooden rib by placing it on the outside of the bowl and using your hand on the inside to gently press the clay up against it. Use a slow stroking movement from the base of the wall to the rim. As the rib cleans away the slip from the outside you may see a little of the grey clay emerging. Don't worry if you don't; sometimes you won't see any of the colour until you carve into it.

8 Use a sponge or chamois leather to smooth off the rim.

9 Cut a notch at the base of the bowl with your pointed turning tool then run a wire underneath.

CARVING

Leave your bowl to firm up a little until it's not quite leather-hard and keep it on the bat. A wide shape like this is liable to warp if you try to carve it while holding it, particularly when it is at this soft stage. It should be slightly tacky to the touch but the walls should feel stable and not move as you touch them. I carve this bowl when it's slightly softer due to the large tool that I'm using – you'll find that if the clay is too dry the tool will only scrape along the surface.

The size of the tool that you use will alter the feel of the piece. I'm after an unfussy look with a strong, deliberate pattern so I'm using a large loop tool. A smaller tool will give you a much more intricate design.

1 Using the rounded end of your loop tool, confidently cut down the wall of your bowl from top to bottom. Support from the inside as you go. Placing your bat on a banding wheel will help you get around the whole bowl easily.

2 Work your way around the whole bowl. Adjust the width of the last couple of cuts so that you're not left with an odd gap at the end. Leave the bowl to firm up a little more – enough that it can be lifted off the bat easily.

3 I find it works best to turn this bowl after carving. It neatens up the bottom of the carved lines while it's still on the bat – these can be difficult to get to with your loop tool. Place your bowl upside down on the wheel head and secure in place. Using a turning tool, get rid of any excess clay at the base of the bowl and cut in a chamfered edge. This produces a shadow gap and adds an elegance to the shape.

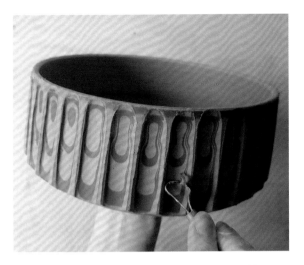

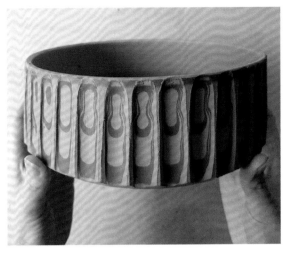

4 I often use a smaller loop tool at this stage to tidy up the carving and even out the depth of the cuts; the pattern will flow around the bowl more naturally if the grooves are cut to the same depth. Be careful though; the key is to know where to stop! It's very tempting to keep going too far and before you know it you've carved right through the wall.

5 Get rid of any large burrs of clay near the base of the bowl with your thumb. I avoid using a sponge here as I don't want to smudge any of the marbling. Don't worry too much about the inevitable smaller burrs of clay; it's easier to sand them off once the piece is bisque fired rather than trying to get rid of them now and risking smudging your design.

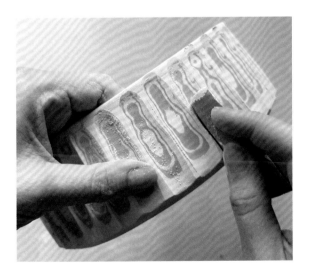

6 Once bisque fired, sand down any burrs or rough edges then clean off any clay dust with a damp sponge.

FINISHES

As all with all my work I like to keep the finish minimal and unfussy. The marbled clay is the focus here and so I leave the exterior of the bowl unglazed. I have glazed the interior with a soft matt black to echo the seam of dark clay that runs through the bowl. It's a good idea to wax the outside of the bowl before glazing the interior, particularly around the rim. This will help to achieve a neat finish where the rim meets the exterior wall of the bowl.

INDEX

AUTHOR
ACKNOWLEDGEMENTS

For my Mum and Dad, for never suggesting a more 'sensible' path, and for supporting me all the way.

And for my boys, David, Edward and Harry – we can talk about something else now.